THE FEMALE LABOR FORCE
IN THE UNITED STATES

193

The Female Labor Force
In the United States

DEMOGRAPHIC AND ECONOMIC FACTORS
GOVERNING ITS GROWTH
AND CHANGING COMPOSITION

VALERIE KINCADE OPPENHEIMER

Institute of International Studies
University of California, Berkeley

Standard Book Number 87725-305-6
Library of Congress Card Number 70-629393
© 1970 by the Regents of the University of California

ACKNOWLEDGEMENTS

This volume is based on the writer's Ph.D. dissertation and, as such, owes much to the guidance and encouragement of my committee chairman, William Petersen. Thanks are also due to William Kornhauser, another member of my committee, for his comments and suggestions, and to Kingsley Davis, who encouraged me to work in this general area. I would also like to express my appreciation to Sheila Moses for her editorial assistance in preparing the manuscript for press. Finally, thanks are due to the Population Council and the Woodrow Wilson Foundation for fellowship support while I was writing part of the dissertation.

                                    Valerie Kincade Oppenheimer

Los Angeles, California
November 1969

CONTENTS

LIST OF TABLES

LIST OF CHARTS

Chapter 1

THE CHANGING PATTERN OF FEMALE
LABOR FORCE PARTICIPATION

Introduction

The major goal of this study is to arrive at a satisfactory explanation for twentieth-century trends in American female labor force participation.[1] Women have become an increasingly important segment of our economically active population, but it is still not sufficiently clear why their labor force participation has increased to the degree it has. There are at least two important factors that make it difficult to arrive at a satisfactory explanation of these changes. One difficulty is the result of the nature of the trends themselves; the other is a consequence of the cross-disciplinary character of labor force analysis.

The explanatory problem is complicated first by the fact that the 1900-1960 trend in female labor force participation can really be divided into two distinct trends: those changes occurring in the period covered by the 1900 to 1940 censuses, and those occurring in the post-1940 period. The increased participation characteristic of the 1900-1940 period appears to have been rather gradual, but after 1940 there was an unprecedentedly sharp rise in the work rates of some groups of women. A theoretical problem is thereby created. We either must have two sets of explanatory factors--one to explain the gradual changes up to 1940 and another to explain the rapid increases after 1940--or we must explain why, if the same variables have been operative all along, their effect has been so much more pronounced in the postwar period. The need to explain an acceleration in the rate of growth of female labor force participation should, therefore, guide the whole course of our analysis, and should also provide one crucial test of the adequacy of any theory concerning changes in female labor force participation.

---

[1] The term "labor force participation" refers to the number in the labor force, regardless of the degree of involvement--full-time or part-time. The terms "labor force participation rate" and "work rate" refer to the proportion of the population in the labor force. The "work rate" is obviously not a "rate" in the usual sense of the term.

A second complication in the analysis of changing trends in female labor force participation is related to the need to utilize several theoretical disciplines: demographic, economic, and sociological variables are all important in labor force analysis. Demographic factors are always potentially significant, because the labor force must be drawn from ever-changing population groups with varying demographic characteristics, some of which--fertility, for example--are highly related to female labor force participation. In addition, economic variables must certainly be operant in any situation involving paid employment. Finally, the contribution of sociological variables cannot be ignored. The employment of women outside the home--especially the employment of married women--has generally been related to familial institutions. The relation of occupational institutions to the employment of women is a little-explored but possibly very fruitful avenue of research. As a consequence of the cross-disciplinary character of labor force analysis, the analytical framework employed in this investigation must be broad enough to permit a comprehensive study of female labor force participation. An exhaustive analysis of the subject is probably too ambitious an undertaking at this point, but the framework employed here must not preclude such an analysis.

In sum, then, this study is devoted to an investigation of the gradual 1900-1940 changes and the sharp 1940-1960 changes in female labor force participation in the United States, within the context of a framework that permits the relevant demographic, economic, and sociological variables to come into play. To begin with, however, it is important to have a clear idea of those trends in female labor force participation which require explanation.

The Female Work Rate as a Whole

The precise nature of the overall trend in female labor force participation prior to 1940 is open to some controversy. In general, the decennial censuses indicate a gradual increase in the female work rate between 1900 and 1940 (Table 1.1). The 1910 enumeration, however, does not fit in with this smooth progression, for it is higher than the 1920 and 1930 rates and just under the rate for 1940. The question that immediately comes to mind, of course, is whether there really was such a sharp fluctuation in the proportion of women working in 1910. If so, what could account for it? If not, do inadequacies in the data for the censuses neighboring 1910 account for those anomalous results, or was the 1910 census out of line in some way?

The standard interpretation of what happened is that there actually was a steady increase in female labor force participation, as the 1900, 1920, 1930, and 1940 figures indicate,

Table 1.1

DECENNIAL CENSUS DATA ON THE FEMALE LABOR FORCE:
1900-1960

	1900	1910	1920	1930	1940	1950	1960
Percent of women 14 years and older in labor force[a]	20.4	25.2	23.3	24.3	25.4	29.0	34.5
Percent change during previous decade		+23.5	-7.5	+4.3	+4.5	+14.2	+19.0

[a]The 1900-1930 data are for gainful workers. The labor force data presented here are not adjusted--i.e., they are the figures as reported in the censuses.

Sources: U.S. Bureau of the Census, 1940 Census of Population: Vol. III, The Labor Force, Part 1, Table 8; 1960 Census of Population: Vol. 1, Characteristics of the Population, Part 1, U.S. Summary, Table 195.

and that the 1910 census "overcounted" women workers and hence was not comparable with the other decennial censuses.[2] The reasons for this presumed overcount are supposed to lie in changes in the instructions to the enumerators in 1910. Evidence for the effect of these changes is seen in the 1900-1910 changes in the proportion of women engaged in agricultural work.

The 1910 instructions to enumerators had made a special point of charging the enumerators not to overlook women workers and to report them as gainfully occupied even if they were unpaid family workers.[3] Apparently as a result of these instructions,

[2]See, for example, Alba M. Edwards, Comparative Occupation Statistics for the United States, 1870-1940, U.S. Bureau of the Census (Washington: U.S. Government Printing Office, 1943), Part II, Appendix A.

[3]For example, unlike the other censuses in the 1900-1930 period, the 1910 instructions caution the enumerator that "the occupation, if any, followed by a child, of any age, or by a woman, is just

3

not only did the percentage of _all_ women who were working go up, but, in addition, the percentage of all women engaged in agricultural work went up as well--and quite sharply. It seems very unlikely that a sharp increase in the proportion engaged in agricultural work--from 3.3 percent of all women, 10 years of age and older, to 5.2 percent--actually occurred, since the proportion of all women living in rural areas declined between 1900 and 1910.[4] For these reasons, it has been argued that there must have been an "overcount" of women workers in 1910, relative to earlier and later censuses.[5] Edwards and others have therefore "corrected" the 1910 figures by assuming that the same proportion of rural women were employed in agriculture in 1910 as in 1900.[6] This very nicely brings the 1910 figures in line with the rest of the series.

Not all students of the problem, however, have been convinced that this interpretation of the 1900-1940 trend and of the anomalous 1910 results is correct. Both Smuts and Jaffe, for example, argue that the pre-1940 increases are not real, but artifacts of the data, and, furthermore, that the 1910 census is not an overcount of female workers but simply a superior enumeration of them, for this census was the only one prior to 1930 that made any special effort to enumerate women workers.[7] Hence, female

---

as important, for census purposes, as the occupation followed by a man. Therefore, it must never be taken for granted, without inquiry, that a woman or child has no occupation" (quoted in 1930 Census of Population, Vol. V, p. 27). The instructions go on to say that "a woman working regularly at outdoor farm work, even though she works on the home farm for her husband, son, or other relative and does not receive money wages, should be returned. . .as a farm laborer" (ibid., p. 28).

[4]U.S. Bureau of the Census, 1910 Census of Population: Vol. IV, Population, Occupation Statistics, Chapter II, "Summary and Analysis of Results."

[5]Ibid. and Edwards, p. 137.

[6]Ibid. and Clarence D. Long, The Labor Force Under Changing Income and Employment (Princeton: Princeton University Press, 1958), Table A-2.

[7]Robert W. Smuts, "The Female Labor Force: A Case Study in the Interpretation of Historical Statistics," Journal of the American Statistical Association, LV (March 1960), 71-79; A.J. Jaffe, "Trends in the Participation of Women in the Working Force," with comments by S. Cooper and S. Lebergott, Monthly Labor Review, LXXIX (May 1956), 559-565.

workers--especially those in categories difficult to enumerate, such as unpaid family workers--were underenumerated in the 1900 and 1920 censuses, and perhaps in later ones as well.[8] Only in the more recent censuses, they argue, do we detect special efforts to include the woman worker. Hence, the 1910 census was probably superior rather than faulty.

Smuts goes on to argue that there is some independent evidence (surveys of manufacturing establishments, for example) that the earlier censuses greatly underenumerated the female labor force. He maintains that, over the years, improved techniques, broader definitions of labor force status, and the redistribution of the female working population into categories easier to enumerate (from unpaid farm work to wage and salary employment, for example) had resulted in an apparent rather than a true increase in the female work rate.[9]

In general, then, because of inconsistent efforts to count hard-to-enumerate workers, and because of several improvements in enumerative techniques, there is a possibility that the 1900-1940 five-percentage-point increase in the female work rate is little more than an artifact of the data-collection process. But, whether or not we assume that there were increases in the 1900-1940 period, there is no doubt whatsoever that the female work rate has gone up considerably since 1940. This is well documented by both decennial census and Current Population Survey data (Tables 1.1 and 1.2).[10] Furthermore, the increases since 1940 have been much greater than for the entire 1900-1940 period. Although there was a 23.5 percent increase in the recorded proportion of women 14 and older in

---

[8]In fact, several of the censuses made an effort to discourage the enumeration of such workers. For example, in 1920 enumerators were instructed that "for a woman who works only occasionally or only a short time each day at outdoor farm or garden work, or in the dairy, or in caring for livestock or poultry, the return should be none [that is, no occupation]; but for a woman who works regularly and most of the time at such work, the return should be farm laborer" (1930 Census of Population, Vol. V, p. 29).

[9]Smuts, p. 78.

[10]Labor force data from the Current Population Survey and from the decennial censuses are generally not completely comparable. The monthly survey data usually yield higher rates of labor force participation, and it is generally thought that these data are better than the decennial census data. For these reasons, census and CPS data are always presented separately. (For a discussion of the two, see Gertrude Bancroft, The American Labor Force [New York: John Wiley and Sons, Inc., 1958], pp. 157-173.)

Table 1.2

LABOR FORCE PARTICIPATION RATES OF WOMEN:
1947-1962

(Annual averages)

Year	Percent of women 14 years of age and older in the labor force
1947	31.0
1948	31.9
1949	32.4
1950	33.1
1951	33.8
1952	33.9
1953	33.6
1954	33.7
1955	34.8
1956	35.9
1957	35.9
1958	36.0
1959	36.1
1960	36.7
1961	36.9
1962	36.7

Source: Manpower Report of the President and A Report on Manpower Requirements, Resources, Utilization, and Training (U.S.
Department of Labor, 1963), Table A-1, p. 139.

the labor force in the forty-year period between 1900 and 1940,
there was a much greater increase in the period half that long
between 1940 and 1960--a 35.8 percent change. In sum, then, although an increase in the rate of female labor force participation may or may not have occurred between 1900 and 1940, a considerable increase most definitely has occurred since 1940, and,
furthermore, these post-1940 increases greatly overshadow even
our highest estimates of the 1900 to 1940 increases.[11]

Female Labor Force Participation and the Family Life Cycle

As one would suppose, the employment behavior of women is
closely related to their family life cycles. However, the nature

[11]The rate of increase for female workers in the 1940's and
1950's is somewhat smaller for CPS data.

6

of this relationship has changed rather dramatically in recent years--so much so that it is these changes, rather than the changes in the overall work rates of women, which stand out most, and require some sort of satisfactory explanation.

There are several ways of showing the extent of female labor force participation at the various stages in the family life cycle. Such detailed information as work rates cross-tabulated by age, marital status, and presence and age of children has only recently become available. Labor force data by age alone, however, are available back to 1900 and give us quite a good indication of both the pattern and the changes in the pattern of female labor force participation (Table 1.3 and Chart 1.1).

In 1900, the highest female work rates were for the young-- in fact, the modal rate occurred for women 20-24, with 32 percent in the labor force. This was obviously the high employment period of young, unmarried women. After age 25, there was first a sharp and then a more gradual decline in the proportion working. This reflected the fact that women were marrying, starting to raise families and, apparently, not returning to work in any great numbers. In 1900, then, it was generally true that, if a woman worked at all during her lifetime, it would be before marriage and children--a very small proportion were working later in life.

By 1940, the rates showed some changes in the degree of labor force participation, but the pattern by age was very similar to that of 1900, except for the much lower rates for young girls, as a result of increases in the average school-leaving age. If we accept the 1900 data at face value, the peak work rate was certainly much higher in 1940 than in 1900 (45.6 percent in 1940, as compared to 31.7 percent in 1900), but the peaks in both years were in the 20-24 age group, when many women were single, or, if married, still childless.[12] In general, then, although the rates for women of every age between 19 and 64 were higher in 1940 than in 1900, the age pattern of labor force participation appears to be very similar to that observed in 1900--a peak at ages 20-24, followed by a sharp, and then gradual, decline in the proportion in the labor force.

---

[12]The median age at first marriage, for example, was 21.9 in 1900 and 21.5 in 1940 (U.S. Bureau of the Census, Historical Statistics of the United States: Colonial Times to 1957 (Washington: U.S. Government Printing Office, 1960), p. 15. In 1940, 39.9 percent of ever-married women 20-24 had not yet borne a child (Wilson H. Grabill, Clyde V. Kiser, and Pascal K. Whelpton, The Fertility of American Women (New York: John Wiley & Sons, Inc., 1958), p. 50.

Table 1.3

FEMALE LABOR FORCE PARTICIPATION BY AGE:
1900-1960

	1900	1940	1950	1960
Median age at first marriage	21.9	21.5	20.3	20.3
Percent of females, 45-64 years old, who were un-married[a]	31.4	29.3	27.9	26.1

Work Rates by Age

	1900	1940	1950	1960
Total, 14 years and older	20.0	25.8	29.0	34.5
14 to 24 years	29.0	30.8	32.5	32.5
14 to 19	26.8	18.9	22.6	23.8
20 to 24	31.7	45.6	43.2	44.8
25 to 34 years	19.4	33.3	31.8	35.3
25 to 29	--	35.5	32.6	35.1
30 to 34	--	30.9	30.9	35.5
35 to 44 years	15.0	27.2	35.0	42.6
35 to 39	--	28.3	33.9	40.2
40 to 44	--	26.0	36.2	45.3
45 to 54 years	14.2	22.5	32.9	46.6
45 to 49	--	23.7	34.8	47.4
50 to 54	--	21.2	30.8	45.8
55 to 64 years	12.6	16.8	23.4	35.0
55 to 59	--	18.5	25.9	39.7
60 to 64	--	14.8	20.5	29.5
65 years and over	8.3	6.1	7.8	10.3
65 to 69	--	9.5	12.8	16.6
70 to 74	--	5.1	6.6	9.6
75 years and over	--	2.3	2.6	4.2

[a]Includes single, widowed, divorced.

Sources: Bancroft, The American Labor Force, Tables D-1 and D-1a;
U.S. Bureau of the Census, 1960 Census of Population: Vol. I,
Characteristics of the Population, Part 1, U.S. Summary, Tables
177 and 195; Historical Statistics of the United States, Colonial
Times to 1957, p. 15; Historical Statistics of the United States,
Continued to 1962, p. 3.

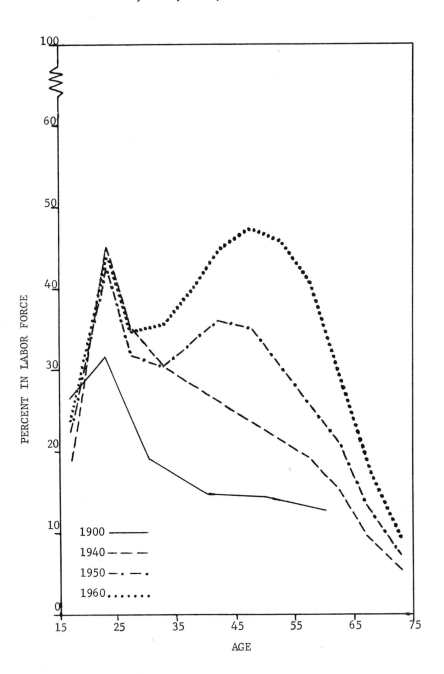

Source: Table 1.3

9

However, the 1900 data probably underestimate the employment of older women as compared to that of younger women. This
is because certain kinds of productive work--unpaid family labor
(especially in agriculture) and piece-work at home, for example--
are particularly prone to underenumeration[13] and are undoubtedly
somewhat more characteristic of married than of single women and
hence of older rather than younger women. Such work was more
important in 1900 than it is today. As a consequence, the census
statistics best reflect the trends and age patterns in paid employment outside the home, rather than the trends in all kinds of
productive work carried out by women. This limitation should not,
however, be a serious drawback in the analysis of the labor force
of an industrial society.

In the 1940 census, labor force participation was cross-
tabulated by marital status as well as by age, and these figures,
therefore, show directly that, if a woman worked, it was usually
before marriage; if she worked after marriage, it was most likely
before the advent of children (Table 1.4 and Chart 1.2). The
highest 1940 work rates were for single women--over 70 percent in
the 20-44 age group were in the labor force. Married women, on
the other hand, had much lower work rates--at no age were as many
as 20 percent in the labor force.[14] The peak work rates for married women occurred in the age group 25-29, and there was a continuous decline in labor force participation after age 30.

The statistics for 1950 and 1960 indicate a sharp increasing break with the traditional pattern of female labor force participation (Tables 1.3, 1.4, and 1.5; Charts 1.1, 1.2, and 1.3).
It is true that in 1950, as in 1940, single women had the highest
work rates and married women relatively much lower rates, especially married women in their late twenties and early thirties,
who were most likely to have young children. As a result, the
work rates were high for young women, and then sharply declined
as an increasing proportion of the female population fell into
the category of married with young children. This has traditionally been the typical pattern of female labor force participation,

_____

[13]See, for example, Louis J. Ducoff and Gertrude Bancroft,
"Experiment in the Measurement of Unpaid Family Labor in Agriculture," Journal of the American Statistical Association, 40
(June 1945), pp. 205-213, and Bancroft, The American Labor Force,
pp. 157ff.

[14]To avoid constant repetition of the cumbersome phrase "married
women, husbands present," it will be understood that, unless otherwise specified ("married women, husband absent" or "all married
women"), the term "married women" denotes only married women
living with their husbands.

Table 1.4

FEMALE LABOR FORCE PARTICIPATION BY AGE AND MARITAL STATUS:
1940-1960

(Percent of women in labor force)

Age and marital status	1940	1950	1960
Married, husband present			
Total, 14 years and older	13.8	21.6	30.6
14 to 19	9.3	19.4	26.0
20 to 24	17.3	26.0	31.1
25 to 29	18.5	22.1	26.8
30 to 34	17.6	22.5	29.0
35 to 44	15.3	26.5	36.5
45 to 54	11.1	23.0	39.3
55 to 64	7.1	13.1	25.2
65 and older	2.8	4.5	6.8
Single women			
Total, 14 years and older	45.5	46.3	42.9
14 to 19	19.7	22.8	23.3
20 to 24	73.1	73.3	73.2
25 to 29	79.5	79.8	79.1
30 to 34	77.7	77.9	79.4
35 to 44	73.4	75.7	78.2
45 to 54	63.5	70.7	76.1
55 to 64	47.2	57.2	64.8
65 and older	16.9	19.7	23.0
All other ever-married women[a]			
Total, 14 years and older	33.7	35.5	38.7
14 to 19	34.6	37.0	35.3
20 to 24	57.0	54.3	53.9
25 to 29	63.9	59.3	58.2
30 to 34	66.6	62.4	62.2
35 to 44	61.9	65.7	68.2
45 to 54	46.6	56.2	67.3
55 to 64	26.8	35.8	47.6
65 and older	6.2	7.8	10.6

[a]Includes widowed, divorced, and married women, husband absent.

Source: U.S. Bureau of the Census, 1960 Census of Population:
Subject Report PC(2)-6A, Employment Status and Work Experience,
Table 6.

CHART 1.2. FEMALE LABOR FORCE PARTICIPATION BY MARITAL STATUS
AND AGE: 1940 AND 1960

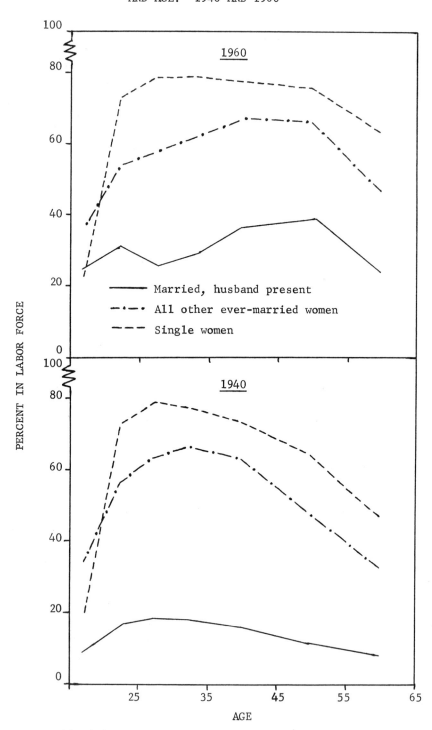

Source: Table 1.4.

CHART 1.3. FEMALE LABOR FORCE PARTICIPATION BY MARITAL STATUS
AND AGE: 1940-1960

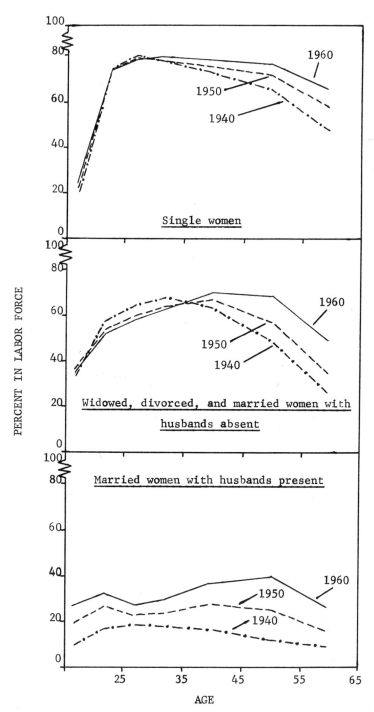

Source: Table 1.4.

Table 1.5

WORK RATES OF EVER-MARRIED WOMEN, BY AGE, MARITAL STATUS,
AND PRESENCE AND AGE OF CHILDREN:
APRIL 1951 AND MARCH 1963

(Labor force as percent of population)

Age of woman, and presence and age of children	Married women, husband present			Other ever-married women[a]		
	1951	1963	Percent change	1951	1963	Percent change
Totals	25.2	33.7	+33.7	39.3	38.5	- 2.0
No children under 18	31.0	37.4	+20.6	35.8	33.3	- 7.0
14 to 24	51.5	55.8	+ 8.3	58.9	57.6	- 2.2
25 to 34	56.0	63.8	+13.9	81.1	66.2	-18.4
35 to 44	45.4	58.8	+29.5	75.5	71.9	- 4.8
45 and older	20.3	31.2	+53.7	29.7	29.4	- 1.0
Children 6-17 only	30.3	41.5	+37.0	61.8	67.5	+ 9.2
14 to 34	35.0	44.0	+25.7	69.6	75.6	+ 8.6
35 to 44	32.3	43.4	+34.4	70.4	70.0	- 0.6
45 and older	23.8	37.4	+57.1	46.7	61.0	+30.6
Children under 6	14.0	22.5	+60.7	37.2	46.1	+23.9
14 to 19	8.7	21.0	+141.4	b	b	b
20 to 24	13.0	22.7	+74.6	30.5	52.6	+72.4
25 to 34	14.5	21.9	+51.0	35.2	42.8	+21.6
35 to 44	14.7	23.4	+59.2	46.9	45.9	- 2.1
45 and older	13.3	24.5	+84.2	b	b	b

[a]Includes widowed, divorced, and married, husband absent.

[b]Percent not shown where base is less than 100,000.

Source: Bureau of Labor Statistics, Special Labor Force Report,
No. 40, Table H, p. A-12.

of course, and the 1950 and 1960 census data do not seem to indicate any radical change. In 1950, however, unlike 1940 or 1900,
the advent of marriage and a family did not lead to a continuous
decline in female labor force participation. Rather, married
women in their late thirties--women usually with school-age children only--started to return to the labor force or perhaps even
entered it for the first time. As a consequence, the 1950 work
rates of married women 35-44 were slightly higher than those for
married women 20-24 (26.5 as opposed to 26.0 percent in the labor
force), and work rates for all women 40-44 exceeded those for
women in the 25-39 age group.

The tendency for married women in their thirties to enter
or reenter the labor force was even more pronounced in 1960. As
a result, for the first time, the age at which the highest work
rates occurred was not 20-24, as it had been in the past, but
45-49, when 47.4 percent were in the labor force (Table 1.3).

These post-1940 increases in female labor force participation are particularly remarkable in view of the fact that there
is some doubt that the 1900 to 1940 changes were as large as the
statistics indicate. For every age group past 35, the average
annual increase has been greater since 1940 than during the 1900
to 1940 period (Table 1.6). For women past 45, the percent increase in the proportion working was greater in the twenty-year
period from 1940 to 1960 than in the forty-year period between
1900 and 1940; and for women 55 and older, the percent increase
between 1940 and 1960 was more than double that for the forty
years before 1940.

While the 1940 to 1960 increases for women of all marital
statuses combined (Table 1.6) have been sizable, the increases
for married women with husbands present have been truly enormous
(Table 1.7). There was, for example, a 139 percent increase in
the proportion of married women 35-44 working, and a 254 percent
increase in the work rate for women in the 45-54 age group.[15]

---

[15]Although it is true that women without preschool-age children
are more likely to be working than mothers of children under 6, it
is also important to note that the increases in the work rates--at
least between 1951 and 1963--of mothers of young children were actually much greater than for other married women (Table 1.5).
There was, for example, a 61 percent increase in the proportion of
married women with children under 6 in the labor force between
1951 and 1963, as compared to a 37 percent increase for married
women with children 6-17, and a 21 percent increase for those with
no children under 18.

Table 1.6

PERCENT CHANGE IN FEMALE LABOR FORCE PARTICIPATION,
BY AGE:
1900-1960

Age	Percent change in the proportion of women working			
	1900-1940	1940-1960	1940-1950	1950-1960
Total, 14 years and older	+29.0	+33.7	+12.4	+19.0
14 to 24 years	+6.2	+5.5	+5.5	0.0
14 to 19	-29.4	+25.9	+19.6	+5.3
20 to 24	+43.8	-1.8	-5.3	+3.7
25 to 34 years	+71.6	+6.0	-4.5	+11.0
25 to 29		-1.1	-8.2	+7.7
30 to 34		+14.9	-	+14.9
35 to 44 years	+81.3	+56.6	+28.7	+21.7
35 to 39		+42.0	+19.8	+18.6
40 to 44		+74.2	+39.2	+25.1
45 to 54 years	+58.4	+107.1	+46.2	+41.6
45 to 49		+100.0	+46.8	+36.2
50 to 54		+116.0	+45.3	+48.7
55 to 64 years	+33.3	+108.3	+39.3	+49.6
55 to 59		+114.6	+40.0	+53.3
60 to 64		+99.3	+38.5	+43.9
65 years and over	-26.5	+68.8	+27.9	+32.0
65 to 69		+74.7	+34.7	+29.7
70 to 74		+88.2	+29.4	+45.5
75 years and over		+82.6	+13.0	+61.5

Source: Based on data in Table 1.3.

Table 1.7

CHANGES IN THE FEMALE WORK RATE BY AGE AND MARITAL STATUS:
1940-1960

Age and marital status	Percentage point change	Percent change
Married, husband present		
Total, 14 years and older	+16.8	+121.7
14 to 19	+16.7	+179.6
20 to 24	+13.8	+ 79.8
25 to 29	+ 8.3	+ 44.9
30 to 34	+11.4	+ 64.8
35 to 44	+21.2	+138.6
45 to 54	+28.2	+254.0
55 to 64	+18.1	+254.9
65 and older	+ 4.0	+142.8
Single women		
Total, 14 years and older	- 2.6	- 5.7
14 to 19	+ 3.6	+ 18.3
20 to 24	+ 0.1	+ 0.1
25 to 29	- 0.4	+ 0.5
30 to 34	+ 1.7	+ 2.2
35 to 44	+ 4.8	+ 6.5
45 to 54	+12.6	+ 19.8
55 to 64	+17.6	+ 37.3
65 and older	+ 6.1	+ 36.1
All other ever-married women		
Total, 14 years and older	+ 5.0	+ 14.8
14 to 19	+ 0.7	+ 2.0
20 to 24	- 3.1	- 5.4
25 to 29	- 5.7	- 8.9
30 to 34	- 4.4	- 6.6
35 to 44	+ 6.3	+ 10.2
45 to 54	+20.7	+ 44.4
55 to 64	+20.8	+ 77.6
65 and older	+ 4.4	+ 71.0

Source: Based on data in Table 1.4.

In summary, then, while the tendency is still for young women to work in their early twenties and to retire upon marriage and the advent of children, since 1940 there has been an important change in the work behavior of married women in their thirties and older. Instead of remaining in the home, they have increasingly entered the labor market after their children have reached school age. *Waldman*

One major consequence of the shift in the life cycle pattern of female employment is that it has greatly altered the composition of the female labor force. The growing tendency of women either to remain in the labor force after marriage or to return to it at some point in their married lives has increased the average age of the female labor force (Table 1.8). No longer is the typical woman worker young and single. In 1900, for example, over 70 percent of the female labor force was under 35, as compared to 57 percent of the female population 14 and older. The female labor force was still disproportionately youthful in 1940, though to a lesser extent, but by 1960, only 38 percent of female workers were under 35--just about the same proportion as in the female population.

Table 1.8

PERCENT OF THE FEMALE POPULATION AND OF THE
FEMALE LABOR FORCE 35 YEARS OLD OR MORE:
1900-1960

(Women 14 years old or more)

Year	Percent 35 years old or more	
	Female population 14 and older	Female labor force 14 and older
1900	43	29
1920	47	34
1930	50	38
1940	52	41
1950	57	52
1960	61	62

Sources: Derived from Bancroft, The American Labor Force, Table D-1, p. 203; U.S. Bureau of the Census, 1960 Census of Population: Vol. I, Characteristics of the Population, Part 1, U.S. Summary, Table 195.

The aging of the female labor force has, of course, been
accompanied by an increase in the proportion of all female workers who are married and with families (Tables 1.9 and 1.10). For
example, in 1940 the labor force had a disproportionately small
number of women past 35 who were married--only about 15 percent,
as compared to 34 percent in the female population. By 1960,
however, as many as 37 percent of the female labor force were
married women over 35--almost the same proportion as in the female population. As a consequence, the proportion of women with
children who were working also went up. Between 1951 and 1963,
for example, the proportion of women in the labor force who had
children under 18 went up from 28 to 38 percent, while the proportion of all women with children under 18 only increased from
38 to 40 percent. What all these changes in labor force composition add up to is that, at least with regard to age, marital, and
family status, the female labor force today is not very different
from the adult female population as a whole.

Supply, Demand, and the Interaction of Supply and Demand

The conceptual framework that appears to be the best guide
to the investigation of changes in female labor force participation
is basically an economic framework of supply and demand. In a
slightly elaborated form, it may be summarized as follows:[16]

A. Supply: Factors (independent of demand) that deter-
    mine or influence the supply of women available for
    work.

    (1) Factors affecting the number of women in differ-
         ent work-propensity categories. (Example: Demo-
         graphic factors affecting the number of single
         women or married women without young children.)

    (2) Factors affecting the propensity of women to
         work.

         (a) Factors facilitating or hindering the en-
              trance of women into the labor market.
              (Example: The availability of labor-saving
              products or services.)

---

[16] This elaboration of factors affecting the supply of women to
the labor market is basically a modification of Hazel Kyrk's
statement of the problem. See "Who Works and Why," Women's Opportunities and Responsibilities: Annals of the American Academy
of Political and Social Science, 251 (May 1947), pp. 44-52.

Table 1.9

MARITAL STATUS AND AGE DISTRIBUTION OF THE FEMALE LABOR FORCE
AND OF THE FEMALE POPULATION, 14 YEARS OF AGE AND OVER:
1940 AND 1960

(Percent distribution)

Age and marital status	1940			1960		
	Female labor force	Female population	Ratio	Female labor force	Female population	Ratio
Marital status distribution						
Total, 14 years old and over	100.0	100.0		100.0	100.0	
Single	49.0	27.7	1.77	23.6	19.0	1.24
Married, husband present	30.1	56.3	0.53	55.1	62.1	0.89
Other marital status[a]	20.8	15.9	1.31	21.3	18.9	1.13
Age and marital status distribution						
Total, 14 years old and over	100.0	100.0		100.0	100.0	
Under age 35	59.0	47.7	1.24	37.8	38.7	0.98
Single	38.2	22.8	1.68	15.8	14.5	1.09
Married, husband present	15.2	22.5	0.68	17.9	21.6	0.83
Other marital status[a]	5.6	2.4	2.33	4.1	2.6	1.58
Age 35 and older	40.9	52.2	0.78	62.2	61.3	1.01
Single	10.8	4.9	2.20	7.8	4.5	1.73
Married, husband present	14.9	33.8	0.44	37.2	40.5	0.92
Other marital status[a]	15.2	13.5	1.12	17.2	16.3	1.06

[a]Includes married with husband absent, as well as widowed and divorced.

Source: Derived from U.S. Bureau of the Census, 1960 Census of Population: Subject Report PC (2)-6A, Employment Status and Work Experience, Table 6.

Table 1.10

DISTRIBUTION OF THE FEMALE LABOR FORCE AND OF THE FEMALE
POPULATION, 14 YEARS OLD AND OVER, BY MARITAL STATUS AND
THE PRESENCE AND AGE OF CHILDREN:
APRIL 1951 AND MARCH 1963

(Percent distribution)

Marital status and presence and age of children	April 1951			March 1963		
	Female labor force	Female population	Ratio	Female labor force	Female population	Ratio
Presence and age of children						
Total, 14 years old and over	100.0	100.0		100.0	100.0	
Women with no children under 18	71.8	61.4	1.17	62.4	59.9	1.04
Women with children under 18	28.3	38.5	0.74	37.6	40.1	0.94
Children 6-17 only	17.3	16.1	1.07	23.2	18.7	1.24
Children under 6	11.0	22.4	0.49	14.4	21.4	0.67
Marital status and presence and age of children						
Total, 14 years old and over	100.0	100.0		100.0	100.0	
Single	29.2	19.1	1.53	22.8	20.0	1.14
Married, husband present	48.8	62.8	0.78	57.0	61.0	0.93
No children under 18	27.0	28.2	0.96	25.8	24.9	1.04
Children 6-17 only	12.9	13.8	0.93	19.0	16.5	1.15
Children under 6	9.0	20.7	0.43	12.2	19.6	0.62
Other marital status[a]	22.0	18.2	1.21	20.2	19.0	1.06
No children under 18	15.6	14.1	1.11	13.8	15.0	0.92
Children 6-17 only	4.4	2.3	1.91	4.2	2.2	1.91
Children under 6	2.0	1.7	1.18	2.2	1.8	1.22

[a]Includes married with husband absent, as well as widowed and divorced women.

Sources: U.S. Bureau of the Census, Current Population Reports, Series P-50, No. 39, Tables 1 and 4; Bureau of Labor Statistics, Special Labor Force Report, No. 40, Tables B and G.

Table 1.11

DISTRIBUTION OF THE FEMALE LABOR FORCE AND OF THE FEMALE
POPULATION, 14 YEARS AND OVER, BY AGE, MARITAL STATUS,
AND PRESENCE AND AGE OF CHILDREN:
MARCH 1963

(Percent distribution)

Age, marital status, presence and age of children	Female labor force	Female population	Ratio
Total, 14 years old and over	100.0	100.0	
Under age 35			
Single	16.3	16.2	1.01
Married, husband present	17.6	20.6	0.85
No children under 18	5.2	3.2	1.62
Children 6 to 17 only	3.5	2.9	1.21
Children under 6	8.9	14.5	0.61
Other marital status[a]	3.7	2.4	1.54
No children under 18	1.2	0.7	1.71
Children 6 to 17 only	0.8	0.4	2.00
Children under 6	1.7	1.3	1.31
35 years and older			
Single	6.4	3.9	1.64
Married, husband present	39.3	40.4	0.97
No children under 18	20.6	21.7	0.95
Children 6 to 17 only	15.4	13.6	1.13
Children under 6	3.3	5.1	0.65
Other marital status[a]	16.5	16.5	1.00
No children under 18	12.6	14.3	0.88
Children 6 to 17 only	3.4	1.8	1.89
Children under 6	0.5	0.4	1.25

[a]Includes married with husband absent, as well as widowed and divorced women.

Source: Bureau of Labor Statistics, Special Labor Force Report, No. 40, Tables B and G.

(b) Factors impelling women into the labor market. (Example: Economic necessity.)

B. Demand: Factors (independent of supply) that determine or influence the demand for workers--in terms of the number and types of workers--in jobs that women might fill.

C. Interaction of Supply and Demand Factors

(1) Changes in supply that affect the number or type of workers demanded. (Example: Shortages of young, single women that might operate to shift demand toward older, married women.)

(2) Changes in demand that affect the amount or type of workers supplied. (Example: Increased job opportunities for older women that might attract them to the labor market.)

Utilizing the conceptual framework outlined above, there are three types of explanations that can be suggested for the changes in the female work rates described above. There is, first of all, the possibility that supply factors, operating independently of the demand for female labor, have been the dominant ones in the situation. For example, one hypothesis is that the increased availability of labor-saving goods and services freed many older women from a variety of household chores so that they could go to work, and hence they did. In investigating this hypothesis, it is important to find out whether the improvement in goods and services was so much greater between 1940 and 1960 than between 1900 and 1940 that it can account for the dramatic changes after 1940. In addition, is there evidence that the growth of labor-saving products and services is a cause rather than a consequence of increased female labor force participation? Was the trend, furthermore, all toward making the burden of household work lighter? Might not the rise in fertility, the suburbanization trend, and the decline in the availability of domestic servants all have operated in the opposite direction? Another factor to consider here is the role of demand in the order of events. If an increase in the supply of female labor was the dominant and initiating factor in the situation, then the role of demand had to be a responsive one. The labor market was, according to this view, able to absorb the increased supply because demand adjusted itself to supply. Unless we take the rather unrealistic view that labor demand or its indicator, employment, is simply a function of supply, then the major way this response of demand to supply could have occurred is through the displacement of male workers by female. A further research question relevant to the supply hypothesis, therefore, is whether there is much evidence that the recent growth in female employment can be attributed primarily to the displacement of male workers by female. We shall consider the theoretical status of the supply hypothesis in Chapter 2.

A second possible explanation for the recent increases in the female work rate would emphasize demand as the dominant and initiating factor in the situation. Here the argument might run that for reasons endogenous to the world of work (the growth of clerical and professional occupations, for example) there has been a rising demand for female labor and, in response to this rise in demand, there has been a rapid growth in the female labor force--that is, in the supply of female workers. Important issues here are whether the very idea of a demand for female labor has some meaning, whether we can estimate such a demand, and, if so, whether in fact there was a rise in demand. Furthermore, since the increases in labor force participation have been the most significant for older married women, is there any evidence of an increase in demand for women such as these? Finally, is there evidence that the supply of female labor is at all responsive to shifts in demand? Of necessity it must be, for the demand hypothesis to be valid. In Chapter 3 we shall attempt to define and provide empirical support for the notion of a demand for female labor as distinct from male; we shall also provide an analysis of those factors that promote the sex-labeling of jobs. Chapter 4 is an attempt to further refine the notion of a demand for female labor by breaking that demand down into demands for specific kinds of female workers. Chapter 5 is, in part, concerned with the question of whether there has, in fact, been a rise in the demand for female workers in general, and for certain kinds of female workers in particular. It is also concerned with what the source of such a rising demand might be and takes up the question of whether the female labor force is indeed responsive to changes in the demand for female labor.

A third type of explanation focuses on neither demand nor supply alone as the single dominant factor in the situation, but emphasizes the importance of both. Here the question is whether it is not the particular nature of the interaction between supply and demand factors that has brought about the observed changes in female labor force participation. Most of the information relevant to this hypothesis is the same as for the demand and supply hypotheses, and the difference between them is probably a matter of emphasis. It is, however, the major conclusion of this study that the interaction of supply and demand factors provides the best explanation for the changes in the female work rates, both before 1940 and after. The argument supporting this hypothesis is put forward in Chapter 5.

Chapter 2

SUPPLY FACTORS AFFECTING FEMALE EMPLOYMENT

The Effects of Changing Population Composition on Supply

As we have seen in Chapter 1, two extremely important factors affecting a woman's propensity to work are her marital status
and her fertility. Although there has been a considerable increase in the employment of married women with children, the work
rates of single women are still much higher. Of course, the propensity to work varies according to many other characteristics as
well--for example, age, race, and rural or urban residence. Changes
in the composition of the population with regard to these various
factors have affected the supply of female workers. If there has
been an increase in the proportion of women in categories where
the propensity to work is relatively high--an increase in the proportion of women living in urban rather than rural areas, for ex-
ample--then such a shift in population composition has tended to
increase the available supply of female labor, even if the work
rates for rural and urban women have remained constant. On the
other hand, if there has been a decrease in the proportion of wom-
en in some high work-propensity groups--a decline in the proportion
single, for example--then this shift in population composition has
tended, other things remaining constant, to decrease the supply
of female labor available. What has been the net effect on the
female labor supply of major shifts in American population composition? Has it been to increase the overall work rate, or to
decrease it? In particular, what has been the effect of post-1940
changes in population composition on female work force participation? Can much or any of the unprecedentedly large increase in
the overall female work rate be attributed to shifts in population
composition?

Analyses by Bancroft, Durand, and others indicate that the
net effects of changes in population composition cannot in themselves account for the rise in female labor force participation--
particularly in the postwar period (Table 2.1).[1] Durand found,

---

[1]John D. Durand, The Labor Force in the United States, 1890-1960
(New York: Social Science Research Council, 1948), Ch. 3; S.L.
Wolfbein and A.J. Jaffe, "Demographic Factors in Labor Force Growth,"
American Sociological Review, 11 (August 1946), pp. 393-396;
Bancroft, The American Labor Force, pp. 41-43.

Table 2.1

THE EFFECT OF CHANGING POPULATION COMPOSITION ON THE
LABOR FORCE PARTICIPATION OF WHITE FEMALES:
1920-1960

Factor of change[a]	1920-1940[b]	1940-1950	1950-1960
Change in percent in labor force	+4.0	+3.60	+5.54
Due to change in:			
Age composition	-0.6	-0.61	-1.92
Farm residence	+1.3	+0.89	+0.70
Marital status[c]	-0.6	-2.81	-0.14
All other factors	+3.9	+6.13	+6.90

[a]Multiple standardization with allocations for interactions
was the method used to measure the effect of each variable.

[b]The 1920-1940 data are from Durand, Table 10. These data
refer to native white women only.

[c]The effects of changes in family characteristics were included with the effects of changes in marital status for the 1920-
1940 period. The data for 1920-1940 on family characteristics
refer to changes in the percentage of married women (husband
present) having one or more children under 10 years old.

Sources: 1960 Census of Population: Vol. I, Part 1, U.S.
Summary, Tables 176 and 196; 1950 Census of Population: Vol IV,
Special Reports, Part 1, Chapter A, Employment and Personal
Characteristics, Table 10; Bancroft, The American Labor Force,
Table 22.

for example, that in the 1920-1940 period, the net effect of changes in age composition, farm residence, marital status, and family characteristics was to increase the labor force participation of native white women by only 0.1 percentage points. However, the increase to be explained amounted to 4.0 percentage points (Table 2.1). Bancroft found, for the 1940-1950 period, that the net effect of changes in age composition, marital status, and farm residence was to decrease the labor force participation of white females by 2.5 percentage points. This meant that a 6.1 percentage point increase was left unaccounted for by this analysis (Table 2.1). In other words, there was more of an increase to explain after the demographic variables had been taken into account than before. Such was the case in the 1950-1960 period as well. The net effect of changes in the demographic variables was again to decrease the female work rate--by 1.4 percentage points this time-- with the consequence that a 6.9 percentage point increase was left unexplained. The shifts in population composition cannot account for the increased female work rate primarily because trends in marriage and age structure have operated to put higher proportions of white women into categories which usually have lower rates. The negative effect of these variables has far outweighed the positive effect of continued urbanization.

In general, then, while such demographic analyses of the effects of changes in population composition may be invaluable, they have obviously not been of much positive value in accounting for the increase in female labor force participation. The primary explanation must lie in some account of why the propensity of women to work has changed.[2]

Factors Affecting the Propensity of Women to Work

Conditions Forcing Women to Work

Discussions of the significance of factors forcing women into the labor market have traditionally revolved around the nature of the relationship between income or wages and the supply of labor. In general, it has been argued that wages have two effects on the supply of labor. First, higher wages cause the worker to take some of his higher income in the form of more leisure, and therefore lessen his labor force participation. This effect is

---

[2] Bancroft, p. 42. However, as we shall see in Chapter 5, a demographic analysis of the effects of changing population composition can be put forth to account for the changing pattern of female labor force participation, provided it can be related to the change in work propensities.

called the "income effect." Second, wage rises raise the price or cost of leisure to the worker, so that he is tempted to work more rather than less. This is called the "price" or "substitution" effect. The question is which effect triumphs--if the income effect, then we have a backward-sloping labor supply curve; if the substitution effect, then the curve is positive.[3] Long's book The Labor Force under Changing Income and Employment represents a major effort to investigate this issue.

Long starts his analysis with an extension of the pioneering efforts by Paul H. Douglas to investigate the slope of the labor supply curve.[4] What Douglas had done was to correlate labor force and real earnings among 38 large cities at two points in time--1920 and 1930. He found that in both 1920 and 1930, the higher the average real earnings in a city, the lower the overall rate of labor force participation and the lower the labor force rate for males and females separately--the negative correlation being somewhat greater for women.[5] Long extended Douglas's analysis of the same cities to 1900, 1940, and 1950, and obtained generally similar results, with the important exception of 1950. In 1950, the negative correlations disappeared entirely, and very small positive correlations took their place.[6] Unfortunately, such correlations were ecological, and it was hard to interpret what the sequence of events was. Long, however, went on to consider the labor force participation of women by the income of their husbands; therefore, his analysis does not rest on ecological comparisons alone.

Using data from the 1940 Census and the Current Population Reports of 1951 and 1956, Long showed that the higher the husband's

---

[3] Clarence D. Long, "Comment," on Jacob Mincer's article "Labor Force Participation of Married Women: A Study of Labor Supply," in National Bureau of Economic Research, Aspects of Labor Economics (Princeton: Princeton University Press, 1962), p. 99.

[4] The Theory of Wages (New York: The Macmillan Co., 1934), Ch. XI; and (with Erika H. Schoenberg) "Studies in the Supply Curve of Labor," Journal of Political Economy (February 1937), pp. 45-79.

[5] Where appropriate, the rates were standardized for changes in age and sex composition.

[6] Long, The Labor Force, pp. 54-57. Long went on to consider whether a whole host of factors may have affected the correlations in one way or another (pp. 63ff.)--for example, whether the inverse associations were the spurious result of concentration of colored persons in certain low-income cities. (They were not.)

income, the lower the labor force participation of the wife--with
or without young children, white or nonwhite, older or younger.[7]
This phenomenon is well-known by now, of course, but it lends support to the theory of the backward-bending labor supply curve.
Long concluded, therefore, that there was a considerable body of
evidence to support the theory that people--and especially women--
work less as real wages increase.

The negative association between female labor force participation and income is no longer so uniform, however. For example, in March 1963 the labor force participation of women 14-
34, and 55 and over with no children under 18, was __higher__ the
greater the husband's income, up to the $7,000-or-over bracket.
In addition, there were some reversals for women with children
6-17 only.[8] Even in the 1951 and 1956 data Long used, there were
peculiarities. For example, the decline in the labor force participation of women did not progress in a very orderly fashion
from income group to income group.[9] An additional problem was
that all the evidence came from "moment-of-time" studies, while
the proposition to be tested was that __rises__ in real income lead
to a decline in female labor force participation. The important
question, then, is what happens over time. What Long found, of
course, was that real income increased as well as female labor
force participation (Table 2.2).[10] Given the considerable rise
in real income since 1940, it is hard to see how the increased
labor force participation of women can be attributed to factors
that __force__ women into the labor market. With respect to supply
factors that might have had some effect, this explanation for the
rise in the female work rate is, then, probably the least satisfactory of all.

Conditions Facilitating or Hindering Labor Force Participation

Declines in the Burden of Household Work. A popular and
convenient explanation for the increases in female employment--es-
pecially that of married women--is that the burden of household
work has greatly declined, freeing women for labor force participation. Now there is little doubt that there has been a tremendous

---

[7]__Ibid.__, pp. 88ff. Long used the monthly population data because the 1950 census data were not available at that time.

[8]U.S. Bureau of Labor Statistics, __Special Labor Force Report__,
No. 40, 1963, Table L.

[9]Long, __The Labor Force__, p. 89.

[10]__Ibid.__, Ch. 6, pp. 97-116.

Table 2.2

DISPOSABLE PER CAPITA PERSONAL INCOME IN 1964 PRICES:
1940-1960

Year	Income
1940	$1,329
1945	1,743
1950	1,743
1955	1,896
1960	2,021
1964[a]	2,248

[a]Preliminary.

Source: U.S. Bureau of the Census, Statistical Abstract of the United States, 1965, p. 331.

increase in the availability and quality of labor-saving goods and services on the market. Nor can it be doubted--difficult as it is to document the relationship--that these facilitate the employment of married women. The crucial question, however, is whether this factor is a sufficient condition for increases in female labor force participation. That it is not is perhaps indicated by the fact that there are so many women who do not work. Just how much, then, can declines in the burden of household work explain? In particular, can shifts in the burden of home responsibilities explain the enormous 1940-1950 and 1950-1960 increases in the work rates of married women? If they are to provide such an explanation, it seems to me that it must be shown that the declines in the burden of home responsibilities in the 1940-1960 period were much greater than in the 1900-1940 period, for it is in the 1940-1960 period that a really radical shift in the labor market behavior of married women occurred. Without seriously questioning the overall significance of declines in the burden of home responsibilities, then, this analysis will pay particular attention to the adequacy of this explanation for the 1940-1960 changes.

The enormous increase in the availability of labor-saving products in the past twenty-five years is so obvious to most Americans that advances in the prewar period may have faded into obscurity. However, a brief review of the history of home mechanization from 1900-1940 indicates that the prewar period saw great improvements in the number and variety of labor-saving products available for home care and maintenance.[11]

(1) Electricity: Electric current was a luxury in the 1890's--the first large-scale generating plant did not begin operation until 1896, for example, and most of the power was used for running streetcars.[12] Electricity, the source of power for most modern appliances, did not, therefore, become widely available to the consumer until after 1900 (Table 2.3). In 1907, for example, only 8 percent of all dwelling units had electricity. It was in widespread use, however, by 1940, when 90.8 percent of urban and rural nonfarm dwelling units had electricity.

Table 2.3

PERCENTAGE OF DWELLING UNITS WITH ELECTRIC SERVICE:
1907-1956

Year	All dwellings	Farm	Urban and rural nonfarm
1907	8.0	a	a
1920	34.7	1.6	47.4
1930	68.2	10.4	84.8
1940	78.7	32.6	90.8
1950	94.0	77.7	96.6
1956	98.8	95.9	99.2

[a]Data not available.

Source: U.S. Bureau of the Census, Historical Statistics of the United States: Colonial Times to 1957, p. 510.

(2) The Gas Stove: Giedion says that the gas range was introduced only around 1880 and won acceptance rather slowly. As late as 1910, a catalogue printed in Chicago listed combined coal and gas cooking ranges.[13]

---

[11]The discussion that follows is based mainly on Siegfried Giedion's Mechanization Takes Command (New York: Oxford University Press, 1948), Part VI, "Mechanization Encounters the Household," pp. 512-627.

[12]Ibid., p. 559.

[13]Ibid., p. 538.

(3) <u>The Washing Machine</u>: Around 1900, the hand-cranked washing machine began to replace the washboard. By 1926 it was still relatively expensive ($150) and only 900,000 units were sold that year. By 1935, its price had fallen to $60, and 1.4 million units were sold in spite of the Depression.[14]

(4) <u>The Electric Iron</u>: The electric iron was introduced in 1909. By replacing the flatiron, which had to be reheated on the range every few minutes, it did a great deal to lighten the task of ironing.[15]

(5) <u>The Vacuum Cleaner</u>: It was not until after 1900 that the vacuum cleaner became a portable machine. Before then it was a rather large plant suitable only for hotels, department stores, and railroad terminals. Montgomery Ward first introduced the portable vacuum cleaner into its catalogue in 1917; by 1929, it dominated the market.[16]

(6) <u>The Refrigerator</u>: The largest refrigerator manufacturer did not start producing refrigerators until 1916-1917, at the luxury price of $900. Not until the mid-twenties did the mechanical refrigerator become popular--by 1923, approximately 20,000 refrigerators had been sold in the United States; by 1933 the number had gone up to 850,000; in 1936 it was two million; by 1941 it was 3.5 million.[17]

A look at annual statistics on consumer expenditures for all household appliances shows that, in spite of considerable

---

[14]<u>Ibid.</u>, p. 568.

[15]<u>Ibid.</u>, pp. 571-572.

[16]<u>Ibid.</u>, pp. 586-595.

[17]<u>Ibid.</u>, p. 602. Giedion states that these figures refer to the number of refrigerators in the United States. However, it seems that he really meant the number sold or the number produced, since other evidence indicates that the <u>production</u> of mechanical refrigerators approximated the number of refrigerators Giedion says existed in the U.S. at the various dates he cites. (See U.S. Bureau of the Census, <u>Historical Statistics of the United States: Colonial Times to 1957</u>, p. 417.) For example, Giedion says that in 1923 there were only 20,000 refrigerators in the United States; however, in that year alone, 18,000 refrigerators were produced (<u>ibid.</u>). Giedion states that in 1933 there were 850,000 mechanical refrigerators in the United States, but 1.2 million were produced in that year (<u>ibid.</u>). There are similar discrepancies for the other years he cites.

year-to-year fluctuation and the marked effect of depression and war, the 1900-1940 period saw a considerable rise in the average expenditures on appliances for each household (Chart 2.1). The overall increase in this period was larger than the increase between 1940 and 1958. This is what one would expect, since the 1900-1940 period is much longer. The point is, however, that there was a substantial amelioration of the burden of household work in the 1900-1940 period, as well as in the 1940-1958 period-- yet it is not until after 1940 that we get a radical change in the work rates of married women. If labor-saving devices were the most important factors in the situation, we would have expected something of a gradual shift to this pattern as the mechanization of the home advanced. Yet in 1940, as in 1900, age-specific female work rates continued to decline after the peak at age 20-24.[18]

Other important labor-saving products are processed foods of different sorts--canned, frozen, and so on. Some idea of the growing importance of such foods can be obtained from examining the average per capita consumption of processed fruits and vegetables (Table 2.4). Throughout most of the 1900-1960 period, the increases in the consumption of such foods have been great. Again we see that the 1900-1940 changes were much greater than the 1940-1960 changes.

Still another reason to doubt that the post-1940 changes in the female work rate are due to increasingly greater ease of housekeeping lies in an unquestioned assumption about which is cause and which effect. There is, after all, no _a priori_ justification for assuming that labor-saving devices and services are necessarily a cause rather than a consequence of the increased labor force participation of married women. The proliferation of such products and services may in part be a response to the demand for them--a demand generated by the increased employment of women. (unlikely)

Increases in the Burden of Home Responsibilities. As we have partially documented, it is true that there has been a tremendous increase in the number of goods and services a housewife can now buy to substitute for her own labor. There are canned foods, frozen foods, packaged partially prepared foods of all types, bakeries, laundries, ready-made clothing, and so on. It is also true that the availability of such services has greatly increased since 1940. However, this increase of substitutions for the housewife's labor has been somewhat offset by a decline in the availability and use of domestic labor. In 1900, for example, there were 98.9 private household workers for every 1000

---

[18]See Table 1.3.

CHART 2.1. AVERAGE HOUSEHOLD EXPENDITURES FOR HOUSEHOLD
APPLIANCES: 1910-1958[a]

(Constant dollars per household)

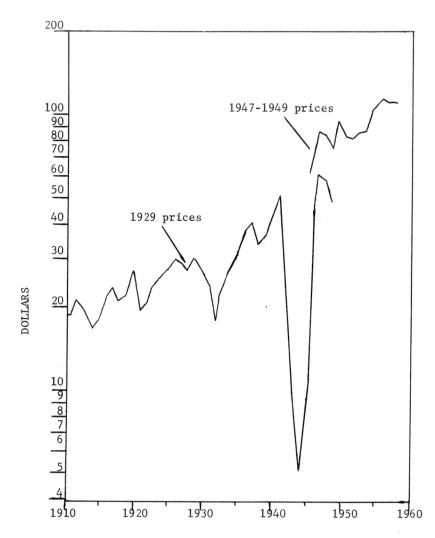

[a]Nonfarm expenditures of individuals as a ratio of the number of
nonfarm households in the United States.

Sources: U.S. Bureau of the Census, Historical Statistics of the
United States: Colonial Times to 1957, p. 15; Historical Statistics
of the United States: Continued to 1962, p. 3; Raymond W. Goldsmith
A Study of Saving in the United States, Vol. I, p. 681; Raymond W.
Goldsmith, The National Wealth of the United States in the Postwar
Period, p. 241.

Table 2.4

APPARENT PER CAPITA CONSUMPTION OF PROCESSED FRUITS
AND VEGETABLES:
1909-1911 TO 1959-1961

(in pounds)

Three-year averages[a]	Processed fruits[b]	Processed vegetables[c]
1909-1911	7.7	15.1
1919-1921	15.9	18.9
1929-1931	18.0	26.5
1939-1941	31.7	35.0
1949-1951	43.0	44.7
1959-1961	48.1	54.0
Percent increase:		
1909-1911 to 1939-1941	311.7	131.8
1939-1941 to 1959-1961	51.7	54.3

[a]Three-year averages were computed to offset annual fluctuations.

[b]Canned fruit and fruit juice, dried fruit, frozen fruit and juices.

[c]Canned and frozen vegetables.

Sources: U.S. Bureau of the Census, Historical Statistics of the United States: Colonial Times to 1957, pp. 186-187; Historical Statistics of the United States: Continuation to 1962 and Revisions, p. 27.

households. By 1940 this figure had gone down to 69.0 domestic workers, and by 1960 it was 34.4 (Table 2.5). The drop was particularly sharp between 1940 and 1950, the period when the greatest changes in female labor force participation were beginning to take place. What about the war?

Along with the decline in domestic help, several other trends suggest that not all changes in the burden of household work operated to lighten the load of home responsibilities—particularly in the crucial 1940-1960 period. Let us consider first the question of fertility changes.

Table 2.5

NUMBER OF PRIVATE HOUSEHOLD WORKERS PER 1,000 HOUSEHOLDS:
1900-1960

1900	98.9
1910	91.4
1920	58.0
1930	66.8
1940	69.0
1950	35.9
1950[a]	34.8
1960	34.4

[a]1950 figures according to the 1960 census classification of occupations.

Sources: D.L. Kaplan and M. Claire Casey, Occupational Trends in the United States, 1900 to 1950, Bureau of the Census Working Paper No. 5, Washington, 1958, Table 6; U.S. Bureau of the Census, 1960 Census of Population: Vol. I, Characteristics of the Population, Part 1, U.S. Summary, Table 201.

For obvious reasons, the presence of young children in the household is one of the prime deterrents to labor force participation by the mother. Young children require considerable care and attention and, unless outside help is available, leave the mother with little time or energy to engage in remunerative activities. The differential work rates discussed in Chapter 1 between mothers of young children and other married women are telling evidence of the difficulty of combining the care of young children with employment outside the home. However, it is well known that although fertility underwent a long-term decline in the nineteenth and twentieth centuries, since 1940 the average number of children ever born to married women has risen (Table 2.6). The child-woman ratio has, of course, also gone up (Table 2.7). Thus, at the same time that married women's employment has been increasing enormously, fertility has not been declining. Hence the burden of child care has not eased; on the contrary, it has been increasing.

The postwar acceleration in suburbanization and home ownership has also operated to increase the amount of time and energy needed to take care of the house and family (Tables 2.8 and 2.9). Houses and yards are more work than apartments and flower pots. They may, in addition, involve the wife in transportation responsibilities she would not have in the center of a large city. For example, she may have to drive her children to school and to

Table 2.6

NUMBER OF CHILDREN EVER BORN PER 1,000
MARRIED WOMEN, 15-44 YEARS OLD:
1910-1960

1910	2,866
1940	1,863
1950	1,859
1954	2,038
1960	2,313

Sources: Wilson H. Grabill, Clyde V. Kiser, and Pascal K. Whelpton, The Fertility of American Women (New York: John Wiley and Sons, Inc., 1958), Table 17; U.S. Bureau of the Census, 1960 Census of Population: Vol. I, Characteristics of the Population, Part 1, U.S. Summary, Table 191.

Table 2.7

NUMBER OF WHITE CHILDREN UNDER 5 YEARS OLD, PER 1,000
WHITE WOMEN, 20-44 YEARS OLD:
1900-1960

Year	Child-woman ratio
1900	644
1910	609
1920	581
1930	485
1940	400
1950	551
1960	667

Source: U.S. Bureau of the Census, 1960 Census of Population: Vol. I, Characteristics of the Population, Part 1, U.S. Summary, Table 47.

Table 2.8

POPULATION INCREASE IN STANDARD METROPOLITAN
STATISTICAL AREAS:
1900-1960

Years	Percentage change		
	Total	Central city	Outside central city
1900-1920	64.9	75.1	48.3
1920-1940	38.2	31.3	51.7
1940-1960	54.9	26.9	101.7

Source: U.S. Bureau of the Census, 1960 Census of Population:
Selected Area Reports, No. PC(3)-1D, Standard Metropolitan Statistical Areas, Table 1.

Table 2.9

PERCENTAGE OF OWNER OCCUPIED HOUSING UNITS:
1890-1960

1890	47.8[a]
1900	46.7
1910	45.9
1920	45.6
1930	47.8
1940	43.6
1950	55.0
1960	61.9

[a] Statistics on the number of occupied housing units are essentially comparable, although identified by various terms--the term
"family" applies to figures for 1930 and earlier; "occupied dwelling unit," 1940 and 1950; and "occupied housing unit," 1960.

Source: U.S. Bureau of the Census, Statistical Abstract of the
United States, 1964, p. 754.

various other activities, and the nearest market may be three miles away--not just around the corner where she can send an eight-year old for a forgotten loaf of bread.

Then, too, although this is very difficult to document, there has probably been a rise in the standards of home care and in the amount of time it is felt mothers should devote to their children.

All the factors we have just been discussing tend to increase the amount of time it takes to keep a well-ordered home. Even supposedly labor-<u>saving</u> devices may actually operate to increase the amount of time spent on household tasks. For example, a woman who might rarely bake, if she had to buy and assemble all the separate ingredients herself and then hand-mix them, might, when flanked by an electric mixer on one side and a cake mix on the other, feel that she can afford the little extra time and energy needed to put a cake together. In other words, in an age when substitutes for a woman's labor at home can be purchased from the bakery, the laundry, the department store, etc., the greater use of labor-saving devices, or superior equipment in the home, may sometimes paradoxically operate to <u>increase</u> the amount of time a woman spends on housekeeping. The hand-stitched and hand-embroidered dress can no longer compete with the ready-to-wear dress, but the Vogue "easy-to-make" dress, stitched and embroidered on a new zigzag sewing machine, may come to substitute for the ready-to-wear--at least some of the time. The affluent society is thus a society where there are many choices open to a woman--she can substitute products and services of others for her own efforts, or she can, with the aid of modern conveniences to increase her productivity, substitute her labor for goods and services available on the market. This latter alternative obviously competes with labor force participation. In a complex industrial society such as ours, then, continued mechanization of the home and the ever-increasing availability of "labor-saving" products and services does not inevitably lead to less time spent on home and family care.

Attitudes

A major set of factors facilitating or hindering, encouraging or discouraging, female employment are familial norms regarding the desirability of women's employment outside the home. An important question to settle, then, in trying to account for increases in female labor force participation is whether they can be attributed, in whole or in part, to changes in attitudes towards the propriety of women working.

<u>Succession of Generations as a Mechanism of Change</u>. Durand argued that one important factor promoting the increase in female

labor force participation was the succession of generations.[19]
He maintained that young women in their early twenties were less
deterred than older women by negative attitudes toward the employment of women outside the home. Hence the younger women were
quicker to take advantage of the increasing opportunities for
gainful employment. As they grew older, Durand argued, the suc-
cessive generations of women retained the greater propensity to
be in the labor force they had developed in youth. In this way,
the increased rates of labor force membership were gradually being
transmitted throughout the age groups from the late twenties to
the early sixties.[20]

This process is most likely a factor in increasing the
propensity of women to work, and it might provide a plausible
explanation of the relatively gradual 1890-1940 increases Durand
was analyzing. However, it is hard to see how the radical postwar shift in age-specific work rates can be accounted for by the
succession of generations. As we have seen, in a ten-year period--
and perhaps less--the whole age-pattern of female labor force participation underwent a dramatic change. The process of succeeding
generations can, at best, account only for a gradual upward shift
in older women's rates, and can never explain the postwar shift.

Although the succession of generations does not seem to
be an adequate explanation for the postwar changes in labor force
participation, this does not rule out the possibility that decisive attitudinal changes took place in the prewar and postwar
periods and that, furthermore, these attitudinal changes might
provide an acceptable explanation of why female work rates rose
so rapidly. Let us, therefore, consider what direct evidence
there is on attitudes regarding the propriety of women working.

Attitudes Around 1900. In Women and Work in America,
Robert Smuts has summarized the attitudes that prevailed around
the turn of the century regarding the employment of women.[21]
Although the evidence is scattered and of uneven quality (from
popular and academic literature, court decisions, actual labor
force behavior, and so on), it seems fairly safe to say that the
employment of women outside the home--even single women--met with
a mixed reception. Many of the middle and upper classes viewed
it with considerable disfavor. It was thought that work would

---

[19]Durand, Ch. 5, "Changing Employment Customs Relating to the
Employment of Women," pp. 122-136.

[20]I have not gone into his evidence here, but Durand devotes
all of Ch. 5 to a statistical support of this thesis.

[21]New York: Columbia University Press, 1959.

expose young women to the harsh realities of the workaday world (and some of the realities of the workaday world were harsh in those days). Furthermore, industrial employment might destroy women's femininity and, by constantly throwing them into the company of men, lead to their demoralization.[22] In addition, it was felt that the employment of wives and daughters was a sign of masculine failure--that it indicated that a man could not support his family.[23] However, as Smuts notes, these negative views toward the employment of women were

> confined largely to the middle and upper classes, and, in many respects,. . .were very much at odds with the experience and common-sense conclusions of most people. A family had to have the means to support its women in sheltered idleness before it could come to believe that this was their natural state. The less sheltered and leisurely a girl's life at home, the smaller was the contrast between life at home and life at work, and the less reason to be disturbed if she took a job. The distance was far greater from the sewing room to the office than from the farm or tenement to the factory. Even among the middle and upper classes many found it difficult to swallow the whole argument for keeping women at home. The constant influx of migrants and immigrants and their steady climb up the urban social hierarchy impeded the development of a strong tradition of gentility. Many successful Americans were still too close to working-class or impoverished agricultural origins to have forgotten how their mothers and sisters worked.[24]

In general, then, around the turn of the century, Smuts argues that

> the employment of girls and women outside the home was greeted with approval as well as misgivings. It was

---

[22]Ibid., Ch. IV, "Women, Men and Work: Values and Attitudes," pp. 110-155. Smuts cites evidence from popular, quasi-popular, and academic sources to support this point. Court decisions were also relevant. For example, in 1903 the Supreme Court upheld an Oregon statute limiting the hours of women's work. The brief in support of the statute declared, "with abundant citations from European and American authorities, that the prevailing ten-hour workday was likely to leave a woman exhausted, her higher instincts dulled, craving only excitement and sensual pleasure"(ibid., pp. 118-119).

[23]Ibid., p. 122.

[24]Ibid., p. 137.

always assumed, however, that most women would be fully occupied at home. The special advantage of industry was that it turned to good use the time and energy of spinsters and young boys and girls who were not fully occupied in household and agricultural tasks.[25]

The attitudes toward the employment of married women outside the home seem to have been more uniformly negative, though again the data are not very good. The main evidence is the fact that most women retired from work when they married. "Even in families which thought nothing of sending young girls to factories, married women rarely worked."[26]

Women who had to work--the widowed and grass-widowed, the women whose husbands were incapacitated or negligent--were usually viewed with pity. The very poor could probably not afford the luxury of negative attitudes toward married women working. However, while there is perhaps no ironclad evidence that most people frowned on married women working outside the home, there is no real evidence, to my knowledge, that such employment was generally looked upon with favor. Certainly, the long workday, in combination with the higher and differently timed fertility[27] and the greater difficulties of housekeeping, militated against the widespread acceptance in 1900 of outside employment as either a feasible or morally responsible activity for most married women.

Attitudes During the 1930's and After. While satisfactory evidence regarding early twentieth-century attitudes toward women working is hard to find, and very seldom of a quantitative or representative nature, there is quite a lot of statistical infor-

---

[25]Ibid., p. 139.

[26]Ibid., p. 141.

[27]Although the average family size has been rising since World War II, this has been primarily due to more women marrying and more wives bearing the first child rather than to a return to the large family sizes which were more typical of earlier cohorts of mothers. The trend has been toward a decline in the proportion of women with large families. See Wilson H. Grabill, Clyde V. Kiser, and Pascal K. Whelpton, The Fertility of American Women (New York: John Wiley and Sons, Inc., 1958), pp. 340-371. A second significant development is the apparent trend toward completing child-bearing earlier in life. Glick and Parke estimate that the median age of the wife at the birth of the last child has gone down from 32.9 years for birth cohorts of the 1880's to approximately 30.5 years for birth cohorts of the 1920's (Paul C. Glick and Robert Parke, Jr., "New Approaches in Studying the Life Cycle of the Family," Demography, II [1965], p. 190).

mation available starting in the 1930's, when the public opinion polls began to take an interest in the subject.[28] The data are not always easy to interpret, but they give us a pretty good idea of what the general attitudes were.

Employment of single women had become so common and so widely accepted by the 1930's that it does not seem to have presented an issue worth investigating any longer. In any event, whatever the situation in the 1930's, it certainly seems safe to say that today, unless a single woman is in college, she is usually expected to work and contribute at least partially to her own support. However, the question of whether married women should work is still something of an issue, and was even more so in the 1930's, and it is about such women that the pollsters were largely concerned.

Questions concerning married women working appeared in at least six polls in the 1930's.[29] On the whole, the general attitude toward women working tended to be quite negative (Table 2.10). Less than 25 percent approved of a married woman working and, depending on the alternatives allowed them, from 40 to over 80 percent disapproved. However, when given the opportunity, a sizable proportion of respondents gave conditional or ambivalent answers, indicating perhaps a certain amount of flexibility--or at least the possibility of it--in their attitudes.

The American Institute of Public Opinion (AIPO) conducted two polls in 1939 which are of special interest because they focused specifically on attitudes of husbands toward their own wives working, rather than on the question of married women in general working. First, AIPO asked two national cross sections of married

---

[28]I am indebted to Betty Stirling for her discussion of these polls and for making me aware that they existed (Betty R. Stirling, "The Interrelation of Changing Attitudes and Changing Conditions with Reference to the Labor Force Participation of Wives," unpublished doctoral dissertation, University of California, Berkeley, 1963). The sources for the poll questions cited in Dr. Stirling's dissertation are, for 1935 to 1946, Hadley Cantril, Public Opinion (Princeton: Princeton University Press, 1951) and "The Quarter's Polls," Public Opinion Quarterly, for polls after 1946.

[29]Fortune had questions on it in one poll in 1936; Gallup had questions in a poll in 1936 and then again in 1939. Finally, the American Institute of Public Opinion (AIPO) had questions concerning the employment of married women in polls taken in 1937, 1938, and 1939.

Table 2.10

ATTITUDES CONCERNING WHETHER OR NOT MARRIED WOMEN SHOULD WORK: PUBLIC OPINION POLLS, 1936-1960

Date	Question	Polling agency	Respondents	Percent		
				Approving	Disapproving	Giving conditional responses
1936	"Do you believe that married women should have a full time job outside the home?"	Fortune	National total:	15	48	37
			Men:	12	54	34
			Women:	18	41	40
1936	Not stated	Gallup	National total:	Not stated	82	Not stated
1937	"Do you approve of married women earning money in business or industry if she has a husband capable of supporting her?"	AIPO[a]	National total:	18	82	--
1938	Same as 1937 question	AIPO[a]	National total:	22	78	--
1939	Not stated	Gallup	National total:	Not stated	78	Not stated
1942	"As things are now do you think married women should work in war industry?"	NORC[a]	National total:	60	13	27

Year	Question	Source				
1943	"Would you be willing to have your wife take a full time job running a machine in a war plant?"	AIPO[a]	National cross-section married men:	32	55	13
1945	Similar to AIPO 1937 question.	AIPO[a]	National total:	18	62	20[b]
1945	"If there is a limited number of jobs, do you approve of married women holding business or industrial job if her husband can support?"	AIPO[a]	National total:	10	86	4[b]
1946	"Do you think a married woman who has no children under 16, whose husband makes enough to support her, should be allowed to take a job if she wishes?"	Fortune	Men: Women:	34 42	46 38	20 20
1946	"Suppose a young couple want to get married, but the man isn't earning enough to support both of them. Should they wait until he is earning enough, or should the girl take a job so they can get married right away?"	Fortune	Men: Women:	44 50	39 33	17 17
1949	"Do you think it is all right for a young woman to work for the first few years of married life to help earn enough so the couple can be married?"	AIPO[a]	National total: Men: Women:	79 77 81	17 19 14	4[b] 4[b] 5

ATTITUDES CONCERNING WHETHER OR NOT MARRIED WOMEN SHOULD WORK (continued)

| Date | Question | Polling agency | Respondents | Percent | | |
				Approving	Disapproving	Giving conditional responses
1960	"There are many wives who have jobs these days. Do you think it is a good thing for a wife to work or a bad thing, or what? Why do you say so?"	Michigan Survey Research Center	National cross-section husbands	34[c]	46[c]	18[c]

[a] Abbreviations: AIPO--American Institute of Public Opinion; NORC--National Opinion Research Center.

[b] Includes a small percentage with "no opinion."

[c] The 34 percent approving include 14 percent who were unqualifiedly favorable and 20 percent who gave favorable replies with qualifications; the 46 percent disapproving include 26 percent downright unfavorable and 20 percent unfavorable with qualifications; the 18 percent giving conditional responses are those who said it depended.

Sources: (1) 1936 and 1946 Fortune polls; 1937, 1938, 1943, 1945 and 1949 AIPO polls; and the 1942 NORC poll: Betty R. Stirling, "The Interrelation of Changing Attitudes and Changing Conditions with Reference to the Labor Force Participation of Wives," unpublished doctoral dissertation, University of California, Berkeley, 1963, Appendix B; (2) 1936 and 1939 Gallup polls: Ruth Shallcross, Should Married Women Work?, Public Affairs Pamphlet No. 49, 1940, p. 5; and (3) 1960 University of Michigan Survey Research Center Poll: James N. Morgan et al., Income and Welfare in the United States (New York: McGraw-Hill Book Co., Inc., 1962), p. 112.

men if their wives were working. Then they asked the men in one
sample whether they would want their wives to take a job if the
wages were $25 a week; the other sample was asked about a $50-a-
week job.[30] The results were as follows:

Whether to take $25-a-week job

Yes	No	No answer
22	71	6

Whether to take $50-a-week job

Yes	No	No answer
33	58	8

Understandably, a somewhat higher proportion of the sample asked
about their wives taking the $50-a-week job favored the idea.
However, quite a high proportion were still against it. The questions, it is true, are rather artificial because they are so hy-
pothetical, and people frequently do not act as they say or imagine
they will. However, whatever the relevance of these answers to
behavior, they do not indicate a very positive attitude on the
part of husbands toward the employment of their wives--even during
a major economic depression when the wages considered were excellent.

During the war there were four polls which had questions
about married women working (Table 2.10). Here the background
factors were very different. The United States was in a major
war, the economy was booming, and there were severe labor shortages with so many men away in the armed forces. The national
crisis lent a patriotic air to the employment of married women.
Under these conditions, it is understandable that the proportion
who approved of married women working went up--especially when the
question was phrased in terms of the woman working in a war industry. It is illuminating, however, to compare the results of
the 1945 AIPO poll with those of 1937 and 1938, all of which used
similar questions--whether or not the respondents approved of
married women earning money in business or industry if their
husbands were capable of supporting them. It was right after the
war, and war industry was, of course, no longer relevant. If the
wartime experience rather than just the wartime crisis had had
some effect on attitudes, it should have been indicated in the
answers. As it turns out, however, about the same proportion

---

[30]Seventy-nine percent of the men in the sample asked about the
$25-a-week job did not have working wives; the percentage was 82
for those asked about the $50-a-week job. (Questions and answers
as reported in Stirling, Appendix B.)

approved of married women working in 1945 as in 1937 and 1938.
However, the proportion <u>disapproving</u> had gone down--from 78 percent in 1938 to 62 percent in 1945. The high levels of female
employment during the war years may have made some difference,
therefore, by at least decreasing the proportion who flatly disapproved of married women working. However, these results may
only reflect the fact that in 1945 it was possible to give a
qualified answer, while in the earlier polls the answers seem to
have been dichotomized into yes and no. It is nevertheless surprising how relatively little change in attitude is indicated,
considering the enormous wartime increases in female employment.[31]

The surveys taken in 1946 and 1949 are of special interest
because, for the first time, they focused on particular kinds of
married women, rather than just on married women in general (Table
2.10). The results were generally much more positive than in previous surveys. The responses were particularly favorable--and
increasingly so--toward the employment of women in the early years
of marriage. Nevertheless, it is interesting to note that there
was still considerable feeling against the employment of women
with no children under 16, <u>and</u> with husbands capable of supporting
them--66 percent of the male and 58 percent of the female respondents either disapproved of or were ambivalent toward work for
even those married women with the lightest home responsibilities.

Centers's study in 1946 gives us the only indication of
how attitudes toward married women working varied by social
class.[32] (His question--asked of men only--and the replies are
given in Table 2.11.) What is particularly interesting about
Centers's findings is that the most permissive attitudes were
characteristic of <u>middle-class</u> men, for whom the economic contribution of the wife is presumably not so important. Working-class
men and rural men were generally much more negative toward married
women working. Thus, although working-class people were perhaps
most in need of an extra income, their attitudes were the least
favorable toward married women working.[33]

---

[31] The answers given may partly reflect a belief that a major
postwar depression was imminent.

[32] Richard Centers, <u>The Psychology of Social Classes</u> (Princeton:
Princeton University Press, 1949), pp. 145-146.

[33] These results may not be very reliable, however. The class
differences may be partly a result of less authoritarian attitudes generally among middle-class men, and certainly the question was not phrased in terms of the economic contribution the
wife could make.

Table 2.11

MALE OPINIONS ON THE PLACE OF WOMEN, BY CLASS AND
PLACE OF RESIDENCE:
1946

Place of residence and class affiliation	Question: "Do you think women's place should be in the home, or do you think women should be free to take jobs outside the home if they want them?"				
	Replies in percentages:				
	Total	In the home	Outside	Qualified answer	Don't know
Urban					
Middle class	100	44	38	17	1
Working class	100	59	24	15	2
Rural					
Middle class	100	58	28	13	1
Working class	100	63	21	11	5

Source: Richard Centers, The Psychology of Social Classes
(Princeton: Princeton University Press, 1949), p. 146.

In general, polls of the 1930's and 1940's do not indicate
a very wide acceptance of married women working. There seems to
have been some trend toward a more favorable attitude, but as late
as 1949 the employment of married women was by no means generally
accepted. However, it is probably more significant that people's
attitudes varied sharply under different circumstances. When work
was patriotic, such as during the war, higher proportions approved,
and, although there was no great general approval of married women
working in the 1940's, the proportion of respondents who were permissive in this respect was higher--though still not large--for
married women with no children under 16. Furthermore, there seemed
to be a growing approval of women working in the first few years
of married life. This attitudinal flexibility has probably been
an important factor in making possible the great increases in female labor force participation in the 1940's and later. Whether
it has been the decisive factor is another matter.

After 1949, the public opinion pollsters seem to have lost interest in the topic of attitudes toward married women working. This may simply reflect the fact that the employment of married women had become so widely accepted that it was no longer controversial. What is perhaps more likely is that the question of whether or not women would take men's jobs has not been a burning issue in recent years, because the feared postwar depression never materialized. There is, however, at least one national study of recent date, undertaken by the University of Michigan Survey Research Center in 1960, which has a question concerning the employment of married women (Table 2.10).[34] Its data are not quite comparable with those of earlier polls, because the questions are phrased somewhat differently; nevertheless, the 1960 information certainly gives no indication that approval of married women working is widespread among husbands, or that the employment of married women is so generally accepted that we need not question people about it. The low proportion favoring married women working is especially significant when we remember that a high proportion of married women were working in 1960. Although only 34 percent of the husbands had favorable or qualifiedly favorable attitudes toward wives working, 38 percent of the wives in the study earned some income in 1959.[35] Employment of married women had undergone a radical increase between 1940 and 1960, but positive attitudes toward it had not kept pace.

A small, but interesting, study of husbands' attitudes toward wives working was carried out in 1961 by Leland Axelson.[36] He found rather pronounced differences between the attitudes of husbands with working wives and those with nonworking wives. In general, the husbands of nonworking wives were much more negative about their wives working. Most thought their wives should never work, or only in emergencies (96 percent compared to 59 percent for the husbands of working wives), that it was not good for the

---

[34] James N. Morgan et al., Income and Welfare in the United States (New York: McGraw-Hill Book Co., Inc., 1962). The sample was composed of a cross section of the U.S. population selected from the Survey Research Center's national sample of dwelling units. It was supplemented by a sample of low-income families selected from the 1960 Survey of Consumer Finances. Answers were weighted, however, so that the over-representation of low-income families should not materially affect the overall results (ibid., pp. 449-451).

[35] Ibid., p. 106.

[36] Leland J. Axelson, "The Marital Adjustment and Marital Role Definitions of Husbands of Working and Nonworking Wives," Marriage and Family Living, 25 (May 1963), pp. 189-195.

children for the mother to work (95 vs. 58 percent), that the children should have completed school first (63 vs. 34 percent), that wives would neglect their husbands (68 vs. 22 percent), and that they would be poorer companions (80 vs. 21 percent).[37] It is, of course, impossible to tell from these responses whether a husband's more positive attitude toward his wife's work preceded or followed her employment. Nevertheless, the consistently negative attitudes of the husbands of nonworking wives makes it seem doubtful, once again, that attitudinal shifts have been the decisive factors in the post-1940 increases in the employment of married women.

All things considered, it seems highly unlikely that we can attribute much of the enormous postwar increases in married women's labor force participation to a change in attitudes about the propriety of their working. The shift in attitudes does not seem significant enough to have effected such a radical change in work patterns. Husbands have not, on the whole, appeared sufficiently enthusiastic about wives working to have brought about this revolution. The significance of these attitudes does not, therefore, seem to lie in their positive power as independent variables. Rather, it lies in their adaptability to changing circumstances. While attitudes have appeared rather negative, there has been a considerable amount of flexibility indicated. Many of the unfavorable attitudes have been conditionally so, and, in general, attitudes have shown themselves responsive to changing conditions.

In sum, I would argue that, on the whole, people are not unqualifiedly enthusiastic about married women working outside the home, but if the work goals can be defined in an acceptable fashion (as really familial goals, for example, such as raising the family's level of living) and the opportunities for work exist, attitudes are flexible enough to permit a considerable proportion of married women to work. If this is true, however, we must seek the reasons for the increased labor force participation of married women elsewhere--attitudes concerning its propriety are, at worst, a deterrent (especially for women with young children) and at best, adapt themselves to the fact of labor force participation rather than cause it.

One important reason that people disapproved of married women working--especially in the 1930's--was undoubtedly the widespread view that working married women who had husbands to support them would take jobs away from more needy individuals--men with families depending on them, or single women who must support themselves. That this was a significant factor is indicated by data

---

[37]Ibid., pp. 190-192.

from the 1945 AIPO poll (Table 2.10), the 1937 Fortune poll, the
1939 AIPO poll, and, to a lesser extent, the 1960 University of
Michigan survey (Table 2.12). Was this the main reason people
disapproved of married women working, or were there other reasons
as important? While the fear that women would take men's jobs
was certainly a major factor influencing attitudes, there is evidence that attitudes regarding women's familial roles were more
important. First of all, while 36 percent of the respondents in
the 1936 Fortune poll who did not believe married women should
have a full-time job said this was because women took men's jobs,
56 percent gave as their reasons that women's place was in the
home or that children would be healthier and home life happier
if women did not work (Table 2.12). In the 1942 NORC poll, also,
the reasons given most often for negative or conditional attitudes
were that women's familial roles obligated them to stay at home.
Again, in the 1960 University of Michigan survey, reasons given
most often by husbands who thought married women should not go
out to work were those pertaining to their home responsibilities--
78 percent of the husbands against wives working cited neglect
of the children or that the wife's role was in the home as their
reason; only 17 percent gave as their reason that working women
take jobs away from men.

In general, though fear that women take jobs away from
men is a persistent factor in negative attitudes toward the employment of married women, this fear is closely related to the
business cycle--it is more pronounced in times of depression and
tends to decline in periods of prosperity. The most consistently
important factor determining negative attitudes toward the employment of married women is the conviction that it conflicts with a
woman's home responsibilities. There is no evidence that this
conviction has diminished much throughout the years.

Supply and Its Effect on Employment

Before taking up the question of demand, let us close
this chapter by considering the logic of the supply argument a
little more carefully. What sequence of events is supposed to
take place? What, basically, are people assuming about the interaction of supply and demand when they argue that the kind of supply factors we have been discussing are the major ones affecting
female employment? In general, they are arguing that the size
of the female labor force--the supply of women to the labor mar-
ket--determines the employment of women. It is, of course, con-
ceivable that increases in the supply of women might operate
simply to increase the number of unemployed females. However,
this has not occurred--the number of women employed, as well as
the number in the labor force, has been going up. If the major
independent variable is supply, however, then it must follow that
supply determines demand and employment in some way. There are

Table 2.12

REASONS WHY PEOPLE DISAPPROVE OF MARRIED WOMEN WORKING:
PUBLIC OPINION POLLS,
1936-1960

---

(1) 1936 Fortune Poll

The 48 percent of respondents who answered that married
women should not have a full-time job outside the home (see
Table 2.10) gave the following reasons for their answer:

		Percent
(a)	They take men's jobs	36
(b)	Healthier children, happier home life if they don't work	21
(c)	Woman's place is in the home	35
(d)	Woman's labor is cheap, brings down living standards	7
(e)	Don't know	1

---

(2) 1939 AIPO Poll

"A bill was introduced in the Illinois state legislature prohibiting married women from working in business or
industry if their husbands earn more than $1,600 a year.
Would you approve such a law in this state?"

	Yes	Yes if	No	No opinion and no answer
National total	67	7	23	3
Married men	68	7	22	3
Single men	67	6	23	4
Widowed and divorced men	71	12	16	1
Married women	65	8	24	3
Single women	58	5	36	1
Widowed and divorced women	68	9	16	7

REASONS WHY PEOPLE DISAPPROVE OF MARRIED WOMEN WORKING (continued)

---

(3) 1939 AIPO Poll

A similar bill was introduced in the Massachusetts legislature. This bill used $1,000 instead of $1,600.

	Yes	Yes if	No	No opinion and no answer
National total	56	10	31	3

---

(4) 1942 NORC Poll

Twenty-four percent of respondents replied it "depended," and 13 percent said "no" to the question: "As things are now, do you think married women should work in war industry?" Those saying "no" and it "depended" were further asked:

(a) "On what does it depend?" (Asked of the 24 percent)

Children and home ties	50	
If needed or drafted	29	
Not if husband can support	8	
If husband is in service	8	(Some gave more
Financial reasons	8	than one answer)
If they want to	4	
Miscellaneous	8	

(b) "Why not?" (Asked of the 13 percent)

Woman's place is in home	46	
Too many single unemployed	31	(Some gave more
Labor shortage not severe		than one answer)
enough	15	
Miscellaneous	15	

---

(5) 1946 Fortune Poll

"On the whole, who do you think has the more interesting time: a woman with a full-time job or a woman running a home?"

	Job	Home	No difference	Don't know
Men	27	49	8	15
Women	32	50	8	10

REASONS WHY PEOPLE DISAPPROVE OF MARRIED WOMEN WORKING (continued)

---

(6) 1960 Michigan Survey Research Center Poll

Husbands were asked for reasons why they were for or against married women working (see Table 2.10 for question).

(a) Reasons Why Favor Wife Working

	Percent of husbands favoring	Percent of all husbands
Supplemental income	63	19
Security--might be essential if husband disabled, dead	6	4
Wife would get bored staying at home	16	7
Other	15	

(b) Reasons Why Against Wife Working

	Percent of husbands favoring	Percent of all husbands
Neglect of children	40	27
Woman's role to be at home and husband's responsibility to support wife	38	15
Working women take jobs away from men	17	8
Other	5	

Sources: (1) 1936 and 1946 _Fortune_ Polls, 1939 AIPO Polls; Betty R. Stirling, "The Interrelation of Changing Attitudes and Changing Conditions," Appendix B; and (2) The 1960 University of Michigan Survey Research Center Poll: James N. Morgan _et al._, _Income and Welfare_, pp. 112-113.

two main ways it can do this. On the one hand, the demand for
labor can be simply a function of the supply. While it is undoubtedly true that the supply of a given kind of labor has some
effect on the demand for that labor and on employment (the best
example of this is probably domestic servants), it seems incred-
ible to argue that employment is solely a result of the supply
of labor. Surely there are a whole host of factors affecting
demand and employment that are independent of labor supply. The
composition of product demand, for example, must certainly affect
employment in certain industries. This, in turn, affects the
type of labor demanded. Second, if employment were simply a
function of supply, unemployment would never exist. Furthermore,
it hardly seems likely that the rise in female employment can be
accounted for merely by the flooding of the labor market with a
supply of female labor. Wages for female workers, as well as
for males, have been rising in recent years, and this hardly
seems consistent with the view that an increase in supply has
brought about an increase in employment.

An alternative to the theory that supply determines employment is that the increase in the supply of women to the labor
market has resulted in an increase in the employment of women because female workers have displaced male workers. Several writers
have maintained that this is what has occurred. Durand argued,
for example, that technological development led to the substitution of semiskilled for skilled workers in many industrial processes; this led to a reduction in the premium placed on experience and craftsmanship, which constitutes one of the older man's
chief competitive advantages. The expansion of the semiskilled
group provided comparatively little opportunity, however, for
reemployment of the older displaced workers. This was because
the semiskilled operatives were chiefly women and younger men.[38]
Thus, Durand argued that women and youths, used as semiskilled
workers, tended to displace older male craftsmen. In this way
he tried to explain both the rising female work rate and the declining work rates for older men.

There seems to be little doubt that there have been declining employment opportunities for older male workers--the
proportions past 50 remaining in the labor force have been decreasing for some time, and older men tend to have higher unemployment rates than younger.[39] However, Durand's argument that

---

[38]Durand, pp. 112-116.

[39]Ibid., p. 35; U.S. Bureau of the Census, 1960 Census of Popu-
lation: Vol. I, Characteristics of the Population, Part 1, U.S.
Summary, Table 195; U.S. Bureau of Labor Statistics, Special
Labor Force Report, No. 31, Table F-1.

this is partly due to the substitution of semiskilled for skilled workers does not stand up too well.

Whatever the trends prior to 1940, since then the crafts-men-foremen occupational group has been increasing in relative importance, while the operatives group has not been increasing since 1950. Thus the proportion of the experienced male labor force which was in the craftsmen-foremen group went up from 15.5 percent in 1940 to 18.6 percent in 1950, and to 19.6 percent in 1960. The proportion in the operatives group went up from 18.1 percent in 1940 to 20.0 percent in 1950, and then down to 19.6 percent in 1960.[40] On the whole, then, relative to other occupational groups, the skilled group is not a declining occupational category, with the semiskilled a rapidly expanding one.[41]

In particular, Durand's contention that female semiskilled workers were displacing older male skilled workers does not stand up. First of all, Durand provided no evidence to support this thesis. If we look at the relative importance of the operatives category for women, we see that this certainly does not seem to be an expanding field of employment for them. If anything, a higher proportion of the female labor force was in this category in 1900 than in 1940--about 24 percent versus 20 percent. Since 1950, furthermore, the proportion of the female labor force who were operatives went down from about 20 percent to about 16 percent.[42] The displacement of men may have been occurring, but, given the statistics, it is hard to see how it was a major factor in the increasing labor force participation of women. Second, even if the displacement were occurring, there is little evidence that the displacement of skilled by semiskilled workers has been an important overall factor, since 1950 at least.[43] Finally, as

---

[40]Bancroft, p. 209; U.S. Bureau of the Census, 1960 Census of Population: Vol. I, Characteristics of the Population, Part 1, U.S. Summary, Table 201.

[41]It is nevertheless true that certain craft occupations have been declining in relative--and even absolute--importance, although the group as a whole has been expanding.

[42]D.L. Kaplan and M. Claire Casey, Occupational Trends in the United States, 1900 to 1950, U.S. Bureau of the Census Working Paper No. 5, (Washington, 1958), Tables 6 and 6b; U.S. Bureau of the Census, 1960 Census of Population: Vol. I, Characteristics of the Population, Part 1, U.S. Summary, Table 201.

[43]It is nevertheless true that such a displacement can be occurring and not be reflected in these statistics--it may be offset by declining opportunities for women in some operatives

we shall see in subsequent chapters, the major increases for women have occurred in white-collar occupations, not manual work.

Long, too, has argued that female workers have been dis- placing older male workers. Women were able to do this, according to Long, because with their increasing education they were at a competitive advantage compared to older men who had less educa- tion and boys who had not yet achieved a comparable education. Long sums up his view of the situation by remarking that one of the dynamic factors contributing to the changes in labor force participation was

> the dramatic increase in education of the average woman, both absolute and relative to that of older men. In conjunction with the growing need for clerical and service labor, this probably gave women a comparative advantage over the less well-trained and frequently overpaid older worker and the untrained child; and it may account for ability of the market to absorb the increased supply of women.[44]

The main difference between Long's and Durand's views seems to be that Durand thought that women were displacing men as semiskilled operatives, while Long apparently thought that women were displacing older men in clerical work.

Long has, in my opinion, virtually no worthwhile evidence to support this thesis. His argument is based entirely on the following:

(1) The labor force rates of older men and young boys were declining while those of women were increasing.

(2) A lower percentage of men with very little schooling (e.g., below eighth grade) were in the labor force, while

(3) The more educated women (particularly those with a college degree) were most likely to be in the labor force.[45]

---

categories, and increases for men in the craftsmen-foremen cate- gory. Nevertheless, in terms of gross figures, this process cannot explain the rapid expansion of the female labor force, though it might explain the decline of the older male labor force.

[44]Long, The Labor Force, p. 31.

[45]Ibid., pp. 174-179. Long attempts to support his theory by graphing the ratio of years of school completed for older men relative to that completed by women of various ages. Against

SUPPLY FACTORS AFFECTING FEMALE EMPLOYMENT

Now the fact that labor force rates for older men were declining and those for women increasing is no evidence that the two trends were related--that women were "displacing" men. Furthermore, the fact that it was men with an especially poor education who had the lowest labor force rates makes it seem very unlikely that they were being displaced by women. The great increases in opportunities for women have been in white-collar employment, as Long himself noted. It is not likely that many men with less than eight years of schooling were in white-collar occupations, and hence at risk of being displaced by the new female entrants. All in all, Long's argument that women were displacing older male workers, while convenient, is not very convincing.

In general, we see that there is not much evidence to support the view that the rising supply of female workers brought about an increase in female employment because female workers displaced older males. There is no direct evidence that women have been displacing men to any significant extent. Furthermore, the rises in female employment have occurred in occupations where the type of male worker who was supposed to have been displaced is least likely to have been an important element. The increases have been greatest for clerical workers, for example, while the declines have been greatest for older men with very little educational attainment.

As far as younger male workers are concerned, considering the increased tendency to finish high school and go on to college, it seems more likely that women would be replacing such workers rather than displacing them. In any event, the work rates of men in their late teens and early twenties fluctuated quite a bit, and declines in their labor force participation can account for only a minute proportion of the increases in the female labor force in the postwar period (Tables 2.13 and 2.14). Although the work rates of men 16-19 years old declined greatly in the 1900-1940 period, they actually increased between 1940 and 1950. They declined again in 1960, but the decline was so small that the 1960 work rate was higher than the 1940 rate. The work rates of men 20-24 years old also fluctuated in the 1940-1960 period--the rate dropped sharply from 1940 to 1950, and then rose from 1950 to 1960, so that the 1960 work rate was only 1.9 percentage points below the 1940 work rate. On the whole, the net decrease between 1940

---

the plot of such ratios, he plotted the ratio of labor force rates of males to females in the same age groups. On the whole, both sets of ratios go down, but the curves do not move together very closely (p. 180), as even Long admits (p. 14). In any event, whether the ratios move together or not, it is not at all clear what such comparisons tell us.

Table 2.13

LABOR FORCE PARTICIPATION OF MALES, 16-24 YEARS OLD:
1900-1960

Age and year	Number[a] (in thousands)	Percent
16-19 years		
1900[b]	2,855	76.8
1910	3,616	79.2
1920	2,547	68.0
1930	2,564	55.7
1940	2,351	47.4
1950	2,183	51.4
1960	2,613	50.0
20-24 years		
1900[b]	2,689	93.1
1910	c	c
1920	4,121	91.0
1930	4,800	89.9
1940	5,011	88.0
1950	4,553	81.9
1960	4,511	86.1

[a]Gainful workers, 1900 through 1930.

[b]16-20 years old in 1900 and 1910; 21-24 years old in 1900.

[c]Not available.

Sources: U.S. Bureau of the Census, 1960 Census of Population: Vol. I, Characteristics of the Population, Part 1, U.S. Summary, Table 195; 1940 Census of Population: Vol. III, The Labor Force, Part 1, Table 8.

Table 2.14

ACTUAL AND EXPECTED NET GROWTH IN THE MALE LABOR FORCE,
16-24 YEARS OLD:
1900-1960

(in thousands)

| | Growth in labor force: 1900-1960 | | |
	Total	1900-1940	1940-1960
(1) Actual growth			
Male labor force, 16-24 years old	1,580	1,818	-238
Female labor force, 14 years old and over	17,193	7,730	9,463
(2) Expected growth in male labor force if:			
1900 work rates remained in effect	3,348	3,563	-215
1940 work rates remained in effect	--	--	-275
(3) Expected minus actual growth in male labor force, 16-24 years old, if 1900 work rates remained in effect	1,768	1,745	--[a]

[a]Both figures yield a decline in the male labor force, 16-24 years old, in the 1940-1960 period. If the 1900 work rates had remained in effect, the decline would have been 23,000 less than actually occurred.

Source: Table 2.13.

and 1960 in the number of men aged 16-24 in the labor force was
about 238,000. However, even if the 1900 work rates had remained
in force in the 1940-1960 period, there still would have been a
decline in the youthful male labor force--by some 215,000 (Table
2.14).[46] Since the total increase in the female labor force
during that period was approximately 9.5 million, the displacement of young male workers by females seems to have been a negli-
gible factor in the growth of the female labor force after 1940.
It might possibly have been more important in the 1900-1940 period, when the increase in the male labor force 16-24 would have
been about 1.7 million more if the 1900 work rates for young males
had remained in effect. Nevertheless, the increase in the female
labor force in the 1900-1940 period was about 7.7 million, about
6 million more than could be explained by the decline in the work
rates for young males. In sum, in neither the 1900-1940 nor the
1940-1960 period can declines in the youthful male labor force
provide a satisfactory explanation for the enormous growth in the
female labor force. The inadequacy of this explanation is particularly marked for the most recent period, the crucial one as
far as this investigation is concerned.

Summary

In this chapter we have sought to ascertain the extent to
which supply factors, operating independently of the demand for
labor, can account for the great changes in female work rates
since 1940. On the whole, such supply factors do not seem to provide a very satisfactory explanation. Changes in population composition, for example, have operated to decrease the female work
rate, not to increase it. Since the postwar period has been, by
and large, a time of rising prosperity, the explanation cannot
lie in economic factors which force women into the labor market.
Furthermore, as we have seen, the negative relationship between
husband's income and wife's labor force status has ceased to be
consistent in recent years.

Declines in the burden of household work have often been
suggested as the major factor in the rise in female work rates.
However, whether this is true is debatable. There has certainly
been an increase in the availability and utilization of labor-
saving products and services since 1940. However, there is

---

[46] The reason the male labor force would have declined even if
the 1900 work rates had been in force throughout the 1940-1960 period is that the male population, 16-24, declined between 1940
and 1960. The demographic reasons for this decline are the same
for men as for women. See pp. 171ff. for a discussion of these
factors.

considerable question whether the post-1940 improvements have been so much greater than the 1900-1940 improvements that they can account for the greater changes in the female work rate. In addition, such labor-saving devices only _facilitate_ labor force participation, and it does not necessarily follow that women will choose to enter the labor force. There are many other alternatives open to them. Furthermore, there have been _increases_ as well as _decreases_ in the burden of home responsibilities in the past 25 years--the rise in fertility and the trend toward suburban living are two examples. Finally, it seems as reasonable to argue that the great increases in labor-saving devices and services are a _response_ to a rise in female labor force participation as it is to argue that they are a _cause_ of the rising work rate.

Another set of factors affecting the supply of female workers consists of the attitudes of relatives, friends, and the community regarding the general desirability of female labor force participation. We have seen, however, that there is not much evidence of a rising tide of enthusiasm with respect to married women working. Attitudes seem to have adapted themselves to the fact of increased work rates, rather than to have initiated these increases.

Finally, we have seen that the only way supply can have been the dominant factor in the postwar changes is if women had displaced male workers on a massive scale. However, there is little evidence that this has occurred.

That supply factors alone fail to account for the postwar rise in the female work rate, or the great changes in the age pattern of labor force participation, suggests that the answer must lie either in the effect of demand factors alone or in the interaction of supply and demand. It is to the role of demand that we shall now turn.

Chapter 3

THE SEGREGATION OF MALE AND FEMALE LABOR MARKETS

In general, the analysis of Chapter 2 led to the conclusion that supply factors alone were not a satisfactory explanation of the extensive postwar shifts in female labor force participation. This negative conclusion leads us to ask whether the
solution does not perhaps lie in demand factors, and the interaction of supply and demand. The problem immediately arises:
How do we talk about demand in relation to the female labor force?
In order to do so, it is clear that we must first make the concept
of a demand for female labor per se meaningful. That is the aim
of this chapter--to show that it is empirically justifiable to
talk about a demand for female labor, difficult as it may be to
estimate the size of such a demand.

The first step is to discard the concept of a single
labor market as being too simple for our needs. It has long been
a commonplace in economics that all workers are not really in
perfect competition with each other for every job in a country;
nor are all employers in perfect competition with each other for
workers.[1] Free mobility of workers among all the different types
of jobs in the country is not possible, if for no other reason
than that "barriers to movement are set up by the skill gaps between occupations and the distance gap between locations."[2] Doctors, for example, do not compete with bricklayers, nor do they
compete with lawyers. Neither do bricklayers in Omaha usually
compete with bricklayers in Philadelphia. So by the very fact
of skill differentiation and geographical distance, relatively

---

[1]For discussions of this general point by economists, see
Paul A. Samuelson, Economics (New York: McGraw-Hill Book Co.,
1958), Ch. 28; A.L. Gitlow, Labor Economics and Industrial Relations (Homewood, Ill.: Richard D. Irwin, Inc., 1957), Ch. 15;
Lloyd G. Reynolds, The Structure of Labor Markets (New York:
Harper and Bros., 1951), Chs. 8-9; Clark Kerr, "The Balkanization
of Labor Markets," in E. Wight Bakke et al., Labor Mobility and
Economic Opportunity (New York: John Wiley & Sons, Inc., 1954),
pp. 92-110. For an interesting discussion of the problem by a
sociologist, see Theodore Caplow, The Sociology of Work (Minneapolis: University of Minnesota Press, 1954), Ch. 7.

[2]Kerr, p. 94.

noncompeting groups arise. Furthermore, there are all sorts of institutional rules which may set off one labor market from another: hiring and promotion policies, union regulations and union-management contracts, may all serve to set off relatively noncompeting groups.[3] In sum, instead of conceiving of the labor market and the demand for labor, a more realistic view is that of a multiplicity of labor markets--some may be only partially competitive with each other, and some wholly noncompetitive.

The relevance of this approach to the analysis of the demand for female labor is this: to the degree that men and women concentrate in different occupations and industries, they tend to be relatively noncompetitive with each other--that is, they are operating in different labor markets. In that case, it is meaningful to talk about a demand for _female_ labor per se--if for no other reason than that there exists a demand for workers in labor markets where females predominate. In this fashion, we can try to relate changes in the composition of labor demand to changes in the demand for female workers.

Everyone knows that there are several "woman's" occupations--nursing and secretarial work, for example, are over 90 percent female. Thus, a demand for nurses and secretaries is, in effect and in the short run at least, a demand for female workers, if for no other reason than that there are few men with the necessary training. How many other occupations exist where women are of such numerical importance that a demand for workers is to a large extent a demand for _female_ workers? Is a high proportion of the female labor force concentrated in such occupations? There may be several occupations which are predominantly female, but if most women workers are widely scattered throughout the occupational and industrial system--in other words, if most are in work situations where the sexes are readily interchangeable--then it probably does not make much sense to talk about a demand for _female_ labor. On the other hand, if a fairly high proportion of all female workers is concentrated in occupations which are predominantly female, then the aggregate demand for workers in these occupations might be taken as a crude indicator of the demand for female workers.

Our first task, therefore, is to consider the degree to which women are concentrated in disproportionately female occupations. To the extent that they are, this gives us prima facie evidence that men and women tend to be in noncompeting labor markets. Our primary concern in this chapter is to show that the idea of a demand for female labor has an empirical justification.

---

[3] For a discussion of such institutional factors, see Kerr and Caplow.

We will postpone the task of trying to get an estimate of the demand for female labor to Chapter 5.

The statistical analysis in the first part of this chapter can show, at best, only that a demand for female labor exists because a demand for workers exists in occupations predominantly made up of women. The second part of the chapter will try to show that the demand for female labor is, in many cases, more direct than this--that different jobs get sex labels which persist through time. For example, it is not just because all secretaries happen to be women that there is a demand for female secretaries. What is in demand is not just a secretary, but a female secretary. This is true for many jobs, and there are several factors which can be distinguished that promote the initial sex labeling of a job, or which help a sex label, once given, to persist. There are, in addition, several factors which lead to changes in sex labels, and we shall make some effort to distinguish these too.

Let us turn first to a statistical analysis of the sex distribution of occupations.

The Concentration of Female Workers in Disproportionately Female Occupations

What can be accomplished by investigating the extent to which women are concentrated in disproportionately female occupations? What conceptual and methodological problems arise?

The objective is to determine the extent to which men and women are involved in relatively noncompeting labor markets. However, the concentration of women in disproportionately female occupations can be only a very imperfect indicator of this. For several reasons it will probably underestimate the segregation of male and female labor markets. First of all, since this study concerns the total female labor force, the analysis will use data on the national level. However, labor markets tend to be local in character. It is possible that a given occupation may be predominantly female in one labor market area but predominantly male in another. The National Manpower Council reports, for example, that in the Midwest "cornhuskers are traditionally women, while trimmers are almost always men. In the Far West, cornhuskers are men and trimmers are women."[4] Occupation and locale are not the only factors which may set off one labor market from another. Industry does to some degree, and there are undoubtedly many other institutional factors that delimit labor markets in some fashion.

---

[4] National Manpower Council, Womanpower (New York: Columbia University Press, 1957), p. 91.

When only the occupational dimension is dealt with, these factors
tend to be ignored, and noncompeting male and female groups may
be combined. For example, the labor market for assemblers in the
automobile industry is probably not the same as the labor market
for assemblers in the electronics industry. The numerical importance of women assemblers in each of these industries was certainly quite different in 1960. Women constituted 67 percent of the
assemblers of electrical machinery, equipment, and supplies, but
only 16 percent of the assemblers of motor vehicles and motor
vehicle equipment. The fact that women constituted 44 percent
of all assemblers is, therefore, a rather imperfect indicator of
the degree to which men and women are used interchangeably in
different assembler-industry combinations.[5]

The extent to which men and women tend to operate in different labor markets may also be underestimated by the use of
census data on occupations, because the number of occupational
categories is necessarily limited. Occupations which are distinct
and which are predominantly composed of one sex or the other may
be combined under one category. For example, according to the
1950 classification system, barbers, beauticians, and manicurists
were all lumped together. Women constituted 50 percent of the
workers of this group. However, when the 1950 data are reclas-
sified according to the 1960 system, hairdressers and cosmetolo-
gists form a separate category, and 92 percent of these were
women. The "teacher" category provides another example. Elementary and secondary schoolteachers were combined until 1960; re-
classification of the 1950 data shows that 91 percent of the
elementary schoolteachers in 1950 were women, while only 75 percent of the combined category were women.[6]

On the whole, therefore, an examination of the occupational concentration of women in the 1900-1960 period will provide us with a very conservative estimate of the extent to which
men and women operate in different labor markets. Keeping this

---

[5]U.S. Bureau of the Census, 1960 Census of Population: Subject
Report PC(2)-7C, Occupation by Industry, Table 2. However, the
occupational breakdown of the operatives category is, to a large
extent, organized on an industrial basis, though there seems to
be a departure from this practice in the 1960 classification
system. The new occupational title "assembler" is one example
of this.

[6]Kaplan and Casey, Tables 6 and 6b; U.S. Bureau of the Census,
1960 Census of Population: Vol. I, Characteristics of the
Population, Part 1, U.S. Summary, Table 201. Hereafter this
census volume will be referred to only as 1960 Census, Characteristics.

in mind, let us now examine the degree to which female workers
are concentrated in disproportionately female occupations.

For any census date, if women were randomly distributed
throughout the occupational system, they would form the same
proportion of workers in each occupation that they form of the
labor force as a whole. For example, in the 1960 census women
made up 33 percent of the entire experienced labor force. If
they had been randomly distributed throughout the occupational
system, they would have constituted 33 percent of the workers in
each occupation. However, in some occupations they were actually
90 percent or more of the workers; in other occupations they were
less than one percent. We can classify every occupation according to the percentage of its workers who are female, and then go
on to determine what proportion of all women workers were in occupations that were disproportionately female. In 1960, this
would be the proportion of the female labor force in occupations
where more than 33 percent of all the workers were women (Table
3.1).

Crude as the data are, they indicate that for every census date from 1900 to 1960 the great majority of female workers
were concentrated in occupations which were disproportionately
female. In 1930, for example, women constituted 22 percent of
the entire labor force, and if they had been randomly distributed
throughout the occupational system, they should have constituted
22 percent of the workers in each occupation. However, 89 percent of all women workers at the time of the 1930 census were in
occupations where more than 22 percent of the workers were women.
If these occupations had each been 22 percent female, we would
have expected them to account for only 35 percent of all women
workers. Thus about 2.5 times as many women as expected were
found to be working in these occupations. The picture is pretty
much the same for every census date, 1900 to 1960.[7]

Table 3.1 gives only a very general indication of the
extent to which men and women operate in different labor markets.
After all, even though it may be disproportionately female, an

---

[7]I do not think it is wise to try to use these data for a trend
analysis. The tables were not designed with this in mind. It is
unlikely that the data, though adjusted, are sufficiently comparable to allow us to trust anything but very large differences.
The more detailed the classification, the more likely were "men's"
and "women's" jobs to be distinguished. I have always used the
most detailed classification available. Thus, the data are not
quite comparable, and changes could easily be the result of a more
or less refined set of occupational categories. In general, the
trend appears to have been toward a more detailed classification.

Table 3.1

WOMEN IN DISPROPORTIONATELY FEMALE OCCUPATIONS:
1900-1960

Year[b]	Females as a percent of total labor force	Disproportionately female occupations[a]		
		Percent of female labor force		Ratio of observed to expected
		Expected in these occupations[c]	Observed in these occupations	
1900	18	21	74	3.5
1910	20	30	83	2.7
1920	20	33	86	2.6
1930	22	35	89	2.5
1940	24	36	89	2.5
1950	28	40	86	2.2
1950*	28	37	85	2.3
1960	33	38	81	2.1

[a]An occupation is considered "disproportionately female" when women form a higher proportion of the workers in the occupation than they do in the labor force as a whole.

[b]The 1960 occupational classification system is not quite comparable to the 1950 system. Data adjusted to the 1950 census are available for 1900 through 1940, but data comparable to 1960 are available only for 1950. For this reason, 1950 data are presented twice: "1950" is according to the 1950 system, and "1950*" is according to the 1960 occupational classification system.

[c]This is the percentage of the female labor force that would have been observed in these occupations if their sex compositions had been the same as the sex composition for the work force as a whole.

Source: David L. Kaplan and M. Claire Casey, Occupational Trends in the United States, 1900 to 1950, Bureau of the Census Working Paper No. 5 (Washington, 1958), Tables 6 and 6b; U.S. Bureau of the Census, 1960 Census of Population: Vol. I, Characteristics of the Population, Part 1, U.S. Summary, Table 201.

occupation where only 35-40 percent of the workers are women cannot be considered a "woman's" occupation. To what extent, then,
are women concentrated in occupations where, at the very least,
a majority of the workers are female? Quite a high proportion
of women workers are concentrated in such occupations (see Table
3.2). Thus, during the 1900-1960 period, between 60 and 73 percent of the female labor force were in occupations where the
majority of workers were women, and between 30 and 48 percent
were in occupations which were 80 percent or more female.

In general, these figures reveal that women and men are
to a very considerable degree concentrated in different occupations. To the extent that occupation is an important factor
distinguishing labor markets, these data indicate that men and
women tend to operate in different and relatively noncompeting
labor markets.

Let us now return to the problem of the adequacy of the
data for the task at hand. To what extent does the analysis of
occupational concentrations of women underestimate the "balkanization" of male and female labor markets? Lack of time and data
preclude investigating this question for the entire 1900-1960
period, but it is possible to undertake a fairly extensive analysis of the 1960 data alone. The following is an analysis of
five occupational categories selected according to their sex composition when classified by industry. The five are:

(1) Clerical and kindred workers: clerical and
kindred workers, not elsewhere classified;

(2) Sales workers: salesmen and sales clerks,
not elsewhere classified;

(3) Operatives and kindred workers: assemblers;

(4) Operatives and kindred workers: checkers,
examiners, and inspectors, manufacturing;

(5) Operatives and kindred workers: packers and
wrappers, not elsewhere classified.

These occupational groups have the common characteristic
that they are very general and hence probably quite heterogeneous.
The sales and clerical categories include all sales and clerical
occupations that could not be classified in other more specific
occupational categories. Each of the operatives categories com-
bines workers in widely different industries with very different
employment patterns--as was illustrated in the comparison of the
different utilization of women as assemblers in the automobile
and electronics industries. An analysis of these occupations by
industry will give us some idea of the extent to which the workers

Table 3.2

PERCENT OF FEMALE LABOR FORCE IN OCCUPATIONS CLASSIFIED
ACCORDING TO PERCENT FEMALE:
1900-1960

Percent-age occupation female	Ob-served	Ex-pected[a]	Ob-served	Ex-pected	Ob-served	Ex-pected	Ob-served	Ex-pected
	1900		1910		1920		1930	
90+	38	7	34	7	31	7	35	8
80+	42	8	48	10	42	9	46	11
70+	54	11	49	11	43	9	49	12
60+	56	11	56	13	49	11	59	15
50+	60	12	60	14	60	15	64	17
	1940		1950[b]		1950*[b]		1960	
90+	34	8	25	7	34	10	28	10
80+	40	10	30	9	40	12	42	15
70+	49	13	46	15	45	14	50	18
60+	61	18	54	18	53	17	56	22
50+	65	20	62	22	66	24	73	32

[a]This is the percentage of the female labor force that would have been observed in these occupations if their sex compositions had been the same as the sex composition of the labor force as a whole.

[b]The 1960 occupational classification system is not quite comparable to the 1950 system. Data adjusted to the 1950 census are available for 1900 through 1940, but data comparable to 1960 are available only for 1950. For this reason, 1950 data are presented twice: "1950" is according to the 1950 system, and "1950*" is according to the 1960 occupational classification system.

Source: David L. Kaplan and M. Claire Casey, Occupational Trends in the United States, 1900 to 1950, Bureau of the Census Working Paper No. 5 (Washington, 1958), Tables 6 and 6b; U.S. Bureau of the Census, 1960 Census of Population: Vol. I, Characteristics of the Population, Part 1, U.S. Summary, Table 201.

in each group are not readily interchangeable--i.e., operate in distinguishable labor markets.

These five occupational groups combined accounted for a sizable part of the 1960 female labor force--about 19 percent (Table 3.3). Although these occupations were disproportionately female, they still had large male components. The proportion of females varied from 41 to 61 percent and, for all the groups combined, was only about 44 percent of the workers (Table 3.3). It might therefore pay to investigate whether a sizable proportion of the female workers in these five groups could be classified into occupation-industry groups that were more predominantly female. One would not ordinarily expect very different sex distributions among industries for an occupational category if the workers or prospective workers are equally competitive.

Table 3.3

SELECTED OCCUPATIONS WITH MIXED SEX COMPOSITIONS: 1960

	Females as a percent of total in occupation	Percent of female labor force in occupation
Clerical and kindred workers:	59	8.0
Clerical and kindred workers, n.e.c.[a]	59	8.0
Sales workers: salesmen and sales clerks, n.e.c.	41	7.1
Operatives and kindred workers		
Assemblers	45	1.4
Checkers, examiners, and inspectors, manufacturing	46	1.1
Packers and wrappers, n.e.c.	61	1.4
Five groups combined	44	19.0

[a]N.e.c. = Not elsewhere classified.

Source: U.S. Bureau of the Census, 1960 Census of Population: Vol. I, Characteristics of the Population, Part 1, U.S. Summary, Table 201.

As anticipated, when each of these five occupational groups is classified by detailed industry, it becomes evident that some of the occupation-industry combinations rely almost exclusively on women, and others hardly at all. For example, in 1960 a relatively low proportion of workers in the clerical group were women in mining, manufacturing industries, and wholesale trade--usually under 50 percent of the clerical workers, n.e.c. On the other hand, quite a high proportion (70 percent or more) of the clerical group were women in retail trade and the service industries.[8] We find that 2.2 and 3.4 percent of all employed women were clerical workers in industries where at least 80 and 70 percent, respectively, of the clerical workers were women (Table 3.4).

The varying degrees to which women are used by different industries is particularly marked for the salesworker category.[9] In 1960, 40 percent of the employed workers in this occupational group were women. However, if we break the group down by industry, we find that very few saleswomen were in manufacturing--only 3 percent, in fact. Nor were women as salesworkers very well represented in wholesale trade--less than 2 percent of saleswomen were in this industry group, and they accounted for only 4 percent of the salesworkers in wholesale trades. Most of the women in this occupational category--about 92 percent--were concentrated in retail trade, but they were not evenly distributed within the retail trade group. They constituted 54 percent of all retail-trade sales clerks, but some retail trades had a very high proportion of women in the sales force--96 percent in limited-price variety stores, for example--while others relied mainly on men: only 3 percent of the sales clerks in motor-vehicle and accessories retailing, for example, were women.[10] In general, 4.3 percent of all employed females (or 60 percent of saleswomen, n.e.c.) were sales clerks in industries where 70 percent or more of the salesworkers were women (Table 3.4).

An investigation of different industry uses of women in the three operatives occupations reveals that here, too, women were very selectively employed. As we have already seen, only

---

[8] U.S. Bureau of the Census, 1960 Census of Population: Subject Report PC(2)-7C, Occupation by Industry, Table 2. Hereafter this census volume will be referred to as 1960 Census, Occupation by Industry.

[9] The reader should be reminded that throughout the present discussion clerical or sales workers as a whole are not being analyzed, but only the residual "n.e.c." categories within these major occupational groups.

[10] 1960 Census, Occupation by Industry, Table 2.

Table 3.4

EMPLOYED FEMALES IN FIVE OCCUPATIONS CROSS-CLASSIFIED
BY INDUSTRY:
1960[a]

Occupational category	Females as a percent of total in occupation	Percent of employed females in occupation	Percent of total employed women in occupation-industry groups where the percent female is:			
			90+	80+	70+	60+
Clerical and kindred workers, n.e.c.	59	8.1	0.7	2.2	3.4	5.6
Salesmen and sales clerks, n.e.c.	40	7.1	0.8	2.9	4.3	4.5
Checkers, examiners, and inspectors, manufacturing	45	1.0	0.2	0.3	0.3	0.4
Assemblers	44	1.3	0.0	0.0	0.2	1.0
Packers and wrappers, n.e.c.	60	1.3	0.1	0.1	0.4	0.9
Total	44	18.8	1.8	5.5	8.6	12.4

[a]Occupation-by-industry data were available for employed women only rather than for the female labor force. Most of the other data on occupations were for the female labor force.

Source: U.S. Bureau of the Census, 1960 Census of Population: Subject Report PC(2)-7C, Occupation by Industry, Table 2.

45 percent of all assemblers were women; yet 67 percent of assemblers in electronics were women. Practically half of all female assemblers were in this one industry.[11] In general, 1.0 percent

---

[11]Ibid.

of all employed females (79 percent of all female assemblers) were assemblers in industries where 60 percent or more of the assemblers were women. A similar situation existed for the packers and, to a much smaller extent, for checkers (Table 3.4).

If we consider these five occupation groups combined, it is evident that quite a lot has been gained by investigating differential industry utilization of female workers. We see that 1.8 percent of all employed women were in those combined occupation-industry groupings that were at least 90 percent female; 8.6 percent of all employed women (46 percent of the women in the five occupation groups under discussion) were in occupation-industry combinations that were at least 70 percent female; 12.4 percent (66 percent of the women in the five groups) were in combinations which were at least 60 percent female (Table 3.4).

If we add the results of this combined occupation-industry analysis to those of the occupational analysis alone, we can significantly increase our estimate--for 1960 at least--of the percent of female workers in occupations which seem to have a predominantly female labor market. On the basis of an occupational analysis alone, it appears that about 50 percent of the female labor force was in occupations staffed 70 percent or more with women (Table 3.2). This percentage can be raised to about 59 percent by adding the 9 percent in those occupation-industry combinations which we found to have 70 percent or more female workers.[12] Furthermore, the analysis of these particular occupations according to detailed industry gives us only a partial idea of the extent to which an occupational-industrial analysis would increase our estimate of the proportion of female workers involved in "female" labor markets. These five categories were probably among the most heterogeneous in the classification system, and were quite large, in addition. This tended to maximize the benefits to be derived from their analysis; but if the analysis of every occupation by its detailed industry were feasible, it would surely be possible to raise still further the estimate of the proportion of female workers operating in predominantly female labor markets.

In general, even though our analysis of male and female labor markets has been, of necessity, quite crude, it indicates a considerable segregation of male and female labor by occupation and industry. There is little doubt that if, on the one hand, a

---

[12]There is no reason to believe that the results would be very different if we had the data to make this analysis for the entire 1900-1960 period. Female salesworkers, for example, have almost certainly always been concentrated not only in retail trade but in retail trade of a certain type.

more refined analysis of occupations and industries were possible and, on the other hand, an analysis of different local definitions of "men's" and "women's" jobs were possible, we would find that the degree of the effective "balkanization" of male and female labor markets has been even more pronounced.

So far, our analysis has been concerned with estimating the extent to which women concentrate in predominantly female occupations. However, little indication has been given of exactly which occupations were the "predominantly female" ones under discussion. Since we now want to take up the question of what factors promote the segregation of male and female labor markets, let us be more specific about the occupations that are involved.

Table 3.5 lists the occupations in which 70 percent or more of the workers were women in 1900 and in 1950.[13] As we would expect, the two lists, together with the proportion of women workers in these occupations at the two dates, reflect the overall changes in the labor force experienced during the fifty-year period. The expansion of work opportunities for women is reflected in the larger number of occupations in 1950 that were 70 percent female or over.[14] The expansion of opportunities is also indicated by the growing numerical importance of jobs outside private household work and factory employment. While 78 percent of the women employed in occupations on the 1900 list (43 percent of the female labor force in 1900) were manual or private household workers, only 33 percent of the women employed in occupations on the 1950 list (15 percent of the female labor force in 1950) were in such occupations.

It is interesting to note that despite all the great changes, however, 14 out of the 17 occupations on the 1900 list also appear on the 1950 list. Their combined significance has been greatly diminished (they accounted for only 36 percent of the female labor force in 1950, while they amounted to 52 percent of the female labor force in 1900), and the numerical positions of different occupations within the group have been rearranged. Nevertheless, on the whole, occupations which were predominantly female in 1900 were also predominantly female in 1950. In addition, women have grown increasingly important in some occupations, such as bookkeeping. In other cases, the occupation itself has become important only since 1900--office machine operators or attendants

---

[13]Data for 1950 rather than 1960 were used because the 1900 data have not been adjusted to the 1960 occupational classification system. (See footnote to Table 3.2.)

[14]This may be partly due, however, to the more detailed occupational classification system in 1950. (See footnote 7, p. 68.)

in physicians' and dentists' offices were not even listed separately in the 1900 census.

In general, the data provide us with considerable evidence of a rather remarkable stability in the definition of those occupations which are "female occupations." The sex composition of occupations does not appear, therefore, to be an accident of labor-market behavior in one year, and open to large fluctuations according to the current exigencies of supply and demand. Rather, there is apparently a surprisingly stable situation whose stability must be explained. It is to a discussion of the major factors which tend to promote this stability that we now turn.

Analysis of Sex Labeling of Jobs: Elementary Teaching

To begin our analysis of the factors which promote the sex labeling of jobs, let us take up the case of one occupation--elementary schoolteaching--and treat it in considerable detail. We can then use this detailed analysis of the factors operating in a single occupation as a springboard to the analysis of general factors leading to the segregation of male and female labor markets. There are several reasons why elementary schoolteaching recommends itself for this task. First of all, it is one of the major professions for women--about 31 percent of all female professional and technical workers in 1960 were elementary schoolteachers.[15] Second, it is typically a female occupation, and has been for some time. In 1950, 91 percent, and in 1960, 85 percent of all elementary teachers were women.[16] Yet, though women are in the great majority, it is an occupation which appears to be in transition as the figures cited indicate. The increase in the number of men in elementary teaching has been enormous in recent years; between 1950 and 1960, for example, there was a 132 percent increase in the number of male elementary teachers, compared to a 41 percent increase for females.[17] Any analysis of sex labeling should try to take into account shifts in sex composition, and elementary teaching provides an example of an occupation where such shifts appear to be taking place. Finally, there is a fair amount of data available on teaching, both from government documents and from private sources, such as the National Education Association.

The Feminization of Elementary Teaching. One major factor in the feminization of elementary teaching in American society

---

[15] 1960 Census, Characteristics, Table 2.

[16] Ibid.

[17] Ibid.

Table 3.5

OCCUPATIONS IN WHICH 70 PERCENT OR MORE OF THE WORKERS WERE WOMEN: 1900 AND 1950

1900

Occupation	Percent of female labor force in occupation	Females as a per-cent of total in occupation
*1. Dressmakers and seamstresses	7.8	100
*2. Milliners	1.4	100
*3. Private household workers	28.7	97
*4. Nurses	0.2	94
*5. Attendants, hospitals and other institutions, midwives and practical nurses	1.8	89
6. Operatives, paperboard containers and boxes	0.3	84
*7. Charwomen and cleaners	0.5	84
*8. Boarding and lodging housekeepers	1.1	83
*9. Attendants and assistants, library	0.0	80
*10. Telephone operators	0.3	80

1950

Occupation	Percent of female labor force in occupation	Females as a per-cent of total in occupation
*1. Nurses	2.9	98
*2. Dressmakers and seamstresses	0.9	97
*3. Telephone operators	2.2	96
*4. Attendants, physicians' and dentists' offices	0.2	95
*5. Private household workers	8.9	95
*6. Stenographers, typists, and secretaries	9.5	94
*7. Milliners	0.1	90
*8. Librarians	0.3	89
9. Office machine operators	0.8	82
10. Sales workers-demonstrators	0.1	82
*11. Operatives--mfg., apparel and accessories	4.0	81

No.	Occupation		
*11.	Operatives-- knitting mills	0.6	78
*12.	Housekeepers and stewards, except private household	0.5	78
*13.	Teachers	6.1	75
*14.	Librarians	0.0	72
*15.	Stenographers, typists, and secretaries	1.8	72
*16.	Operatives--misc. fabricated textile products	0.3	71
*17.	Operatives--apparel and accessories mfg.	3.0	70

No.	Occupation		
*12.	Bookkeepers and cashiers	4.7	78
13.	Counter and fountain workers and waitresses	4.0	78
*14.	Housekeepers and stewards, except private household	0.5	78
*15.	Teachers	5.2	75
*16.	Attendants and assistants, library	0.1	74
17.	Spinners, textile	0.4	74
*18.	Operatives--knitting	0.7	72
*19.	Operatives--misc. fabricated textile products	0.2	72
*20.	Boarding and lodging housekeepers	0.1	72
21.	Dancers and dancing teachers	0.1	71
22.	Religious workers	0.2	70
23.	Operatives--tobacco mfg.	0.3	70

*Indicates that the occupation is on both the 1900 and the 1950 lists.

Source: David L. Kaplan and M. Claire Casey, Occupational Trends in the United States, 1900 to 1950, Bureau of the Census Working Paper No. 5 (Washington, 1958), Tables 6 and 6b.

was that women provided a cheap and relatively plentiful supply of labor, when qualified male labor was neither so readily nor so cheaply available. On the one hand, many districts--particularly rural ones--could not afford or were not willing to pay wages that would have attracted male teachers. On the other hand, in the nineteenth and early twentieth centuries there were few nonmanual occupations open to women, and therefore many women of middle-class status or aspirations were available for teaching, and at a much lower rate than men. On the whole, it does not appear that women displaced men in teaching--though they may have replaced them. Rather, there were so many other opportunities available to native men and teaching was so poorly paid that it simply could not compete.[18]

Another salient characteristic of teaching--even elementary teaching--is that it is an occupation requiring a fairly high level of education compared to that of the general population. It is true, of course, that female teachers in the past did not have either the degree or quality of education expected of teachers today. Smuts, for example, reports that

> most schoolteachers had only six or eight years of elementary education, and it was not until 1907 that Indiana became the first state to require that all licensed teachers be high school graduates. In three of the North Central states, only about 10 percent of the teachers (men and women) during the 1891-92 school year were normal school or college graduates.

---

[18]For a very interesting discussion of the entry of women into teaching, see Thomas Woody, A History of Women's Education in the United States (New York: The Science Press, 1929), Vol. I, pp. 460-518. Edith Abbott also discusses women teachers. She argues that the wages of teachers were so low in the middle of the nineteenth century that there was even trouble finding women teachers. Cotton mills competed as an alternative employment, and "it was very common to find the schoolmistress in the mill for part of the year at least" (Edith Abbott, Women in Industry [New York: D. Appleton & Co., 1910], p. 119). She goes on to report that Horace Mann, in an 1847 report to the Massachusetts Board of Education, "was obliged to call attention to the fact that schoolmistresses were still so inadequately paid that women in many occupations in mills and factories earned six or seven times as much as women teachers. Higher salaries and more permanent employment would be necessary, he said, before school committees could 'escape the mortification which they now sometimes suffer, of being overbid by a capitalist who wants them for his factory and who can afford to pay them more for superintending a loom or a spinning frame' " (ibid., p. 120).

> As Nicholas Murray Butler described them, the
> normal schools were no more than "two-year high
> schools with a slight infusion of pedagogic in-
> struction."[19]

Compared to our day, this certainly is not much, but these younger
teachers nevertheless had a certain basic education and facility
with the English language--an important qualification when European immigrants were pouring into our cities. Furthermore, the
amount of training required of teachers has been steadily rising.
The quality and relevance of this training has been severely criticized,[20] but there seems little doubt that there has been some
improvement in teacher quality since the turn of the century. In
addition, regardless of questions of quality, becoming a teacher
has entailed an increasing investment of training and time. Although relatively few of the teachers in the nineteenth century
completed high school, by 1960 the median years of school completed was over 16 for both male and female teachers, and for
elementary as well as secondary schoolteaching (see Table 3.6).
A sizable proportion of teachers had some graduate training. It
is important to note that the educational attainment of teachers,
whether secondary or elementary, was not only much greater than
that for the experienced labor force as a whole, but it was also
significantly greater than for all workers in the professional
and technical category.[21]

Thus we see that elementary and secondary teachers--both
men and women--spend a considerable number of years in school.
Keeping these training requirements in mind, let us examine the
competitive position of the occupation with regard to income received. What are the monetary rewards to the teacher, or, to put
it differently, what is the price the community has to pay for
such educated workers? Income data reveal a very interesting
variation in pattern between the sexes (Table 3.6). As noted
above, in 1960 female elementary and secondary teachers had completed more years of school on the average than female workers in
the professional and technical occupational category as a whole,
and than the total female experienced labor force. In contrast
to men, however, female elementary and secondary teachers received,

---

[19]Robert W. Smuts, Women and Work in America (New York: Columbia
University Press, 1959), p. 20.

[20]See, for example, James Koerner, Miseducation of American
Teachers (Boston: Houghton Mifflin, 1963), and Arthur Bestor,
Restoration of Learning (New York: Alfred A. Knopf, 1955).

[21]These figures cannot, of course, tell us about the relative
quality of the education received in these different groups.

THE FEMALE LABOR FORCE IN THE UNITED STATES

Table 3.6

EDUCATIONAL ATTAINMENT AND 1959 INCOME FOR TEACHERS, ALL
PROFESSIONAL WORKERS, AND THE TOTAL EXPERIENCED LABOR FORCE, BY SEX
1960

Labor force	Educational attainment		1959 income		
	Median school years completed	Percent with 4 years or more of college	Median income (dollars)	Percent with $6,000 or more	Percent with $7,000 or more
Females					
Elementary teachers	16.4	67.9	4,099	15.5	6.9
Secondary teachers	16.8	88.8	4,492	24.1	13.2
All professionals	15.7	45.8	3,711	14.8	7.5
Total labor force	12.1	7.9	2,333	4.2	7.2
Males					
Elementary teachers	17.0	86.0	5,310	35.6	21.0
Secondary teachers	17.2	92.8	5,966	48.5	31.4
All professionals	16.3	55.8	6,778	60.0	47.1
Total labor force	11.1	9.7	4,720	30.9	20.6

Source: U.S. Bureau of the Census, 1960 Census of Population:
Subject Report PC(2)-7A, Occupational Characteristics, Tables 9
and 25.

on the average, a higher income in 1959 than female workers in
the two other categories. For women, then, teaching appears to
offer somewhat better economic opportunities than exist in other
occupations, though the advantage women teachers have over professional women in the $6,000-and-over bracket is very small,
and is entirely lost in the $7,000-and-over bracket. Neverthe-
less, teaching offers, if not the opportunity for large economic
rewards relative to the other professional occupations, a better
chance of a moderate income. On this and many other counts, we
can assume that teaching recommends itself to women.

The situation is quite different for men. While male,
like female teachers, have been in school longer than workers in
the professional and technical category as a whole, their earnings
do not--as the women's do--compare favorably to workers in the

professions generally. This is particularly true for the elementary teacher, whose earnings are not a great deal larger than for the experienced male labor force as a whole.[22] Although the median number of school years completed by male elementary teachers was 5.9 years greater than the median for all male workers, their median income was only $590 greater. On the other hand, although the secondary teachers had a median of 17.2 years of school completed--only 0.2 of a year more than the elementary teachers--their median income ($5,966) was $656 higher than the median for the elementary teachers and $1,246 higher than the median for all male workers. The added 0.2 of a year appears to have paid off particularly well.

The advantage of the elementary teachers over all male workers appears particularly slight in the upper income brackets. About 35 percent of the male elementary teachers made $6,000 a year or more, but about 31 percent of all male workers achieved this income, and the proportion in both categories earning $7,000 a year or more is the same--21 percent. The income position of elementary teachers is not even as favorable as these statistics seem to indicate, since elementary school principals are included in the category as well. The principals undoubtedly form a rather large proportion of the upper income group.

Thus we see that, on the average, both elementary and secondary male teachers went to school longer than professional workers as a group, but received lower incomes--in 1960 at least--than all male workers in the professional and technical category. This poor economic position was particularly characteristic of the elementary teacher.

The comparison of 1959 incomes for male teachers, the professional category as a whole, and the total experienced male labor force glosses over quite a few important characteristics of the relative economic position of the teacher. Several additional insights can be gained by investigating the situation a little more thoroughly. Which professions or technical occupations had lower 1959 median incomes than teachers, and what are some of the characteristics of these occupations? It should be possible to learn something about the position of teachers by learning about the occupations which appear to be in a worse

---

[22]Many men, however, use elementary teaching as a stepping-stone to administrative positions in education--positions which have much higher rewards than teaching. See pp. 91ff. for a discussion of this point. However, what I am seeking to indicate at the present time are the relative rewards of the occupation of elementary schoolteaching itself, not the expected rewards of men who enter elementary teaching.

position. For example, do these occupations resemble teaching in terms of educational attainment? Are women important components of these occupations? Are there many numerically important male occupations with educational standards comparable to teaching, but with even lower salaries?

There were 50 occupations detailed in the professional and technical category in the 1960 census. Of these 50, 21 had lower median earnings for males than secondary teachers, but only 12 had lower median earnings than elementary teachers (Table 3.7). Only 10 percent of the male professional and technical workers were in occupations with lower median earnings than elementary teachers. Occupations accounting for 88 percent of the male professional labor force had higher median incomes than elementary teachers.

In 9 of the 12 occupations with lower earnings than elementary teachers, the median years of school completed was below 16; in 7 it was 13 years or less. In 7 of these 12 occupations, women constituted the majority of workers. Thus in 11 out of the 12 occupations, the median years of school completed was less than 16, or the occupation was one where women were in the majority. The only occupational group with a lower income which had an educational attainment comparable to elementary schoolteaching but which did not have women in the majority was the clergy, which obviously forms a special case.

On the whole, then, we see that it is either in professional and technical occupations whose workers have a fairly low educational attainment, or in professional occupations with a major female component, that lower incomes than teachers--particularly elementary schoolteachers--are to be found. Comparisons with the professional and technical group as a whole do not, therefore, mask a whole range of male occupations with educational characteristics similar to those of teachers, but with lower incomes.

Our understanding of the economic position of teaching can be extended by examining the earnings of teachers and workers in several other occupations for various age groups (Table 3.8). Although the earnings for workers in different age groups can give us only a very artificial view of the earnings over time of a cohort of workers in an occupation, such data probably indicate what appear to young workers to be the future opportunities of the occupation. As such, they probably substantially influence decisions regarding entry into and departures from occupations.

If we look at the median earnings by age, we see that among the younger workers--those under 25--the difference in median earnings was not large when elementary and secondary teachers were compared to professional workers. However, the relative

advantage of professional workers as a whole increased greatly
with age. For example, although the median income for the professional category as a whole was only $1,421 larger than the
median for all male elementary teachers, male professional workers 35-44 and 45-54 had median incomes that were $1,921 and
$1,923 larger, respectively, than elementary teachers in those
age groups.

Compared to the earnings of professional workers as a
group, the 1959 median earnings of schoolteachers were usually
lower in all but the younger age groups than what we would expect
on the basis of comparisons of median earnings for all ages combined. The economic disadvantage of the teacher--especially the
elementary teacher--appears to be a lifelong disadvantage. We
reach a similar conclusion when we compare teachers to male workers in the managerial category. Many men, of course, plan to use
elementary teaching as a stepping-stone to school administration.
The relatively poor lifetime earnings of teachers may not, therefore, be an important consideration as far as such would-be school
administrators are concerned. However, we are concerned here with
the economic rewards of school teaching, not school administration.
Although the relatively low economic rewards in teaching may not
be a major factor in whether or not males enter the profession,
they undoubtedly are a major factor in the decision to stay in
teaching, or depart for some other occupation such as school administration.

The earnings of teachers compared to those of other professional workers or to managerial workers may be low, but a somewhat different picture emerges when we compare the earnings by
age for male teachers with those of the entire male labor force
and the other major occupational groups (Table 3.8). Compared to
blue-collar workers and clerical workers, the median earnings of
both secondary and elementary teachers were generally quite high.
It is interesting to see how the differentials varied by age.
Among young workers, there was relatively little difference in
median earnings, or the teacher may have had even lower earnings.
However, the relative position of the teacher--particularly the
secondary school teacher--was much better for older workers.
Thus, while the median earnings of 25-34 year old craftsmen and
foremen were $367 larger than those of elementary schoolteachers
of similar age, the 45-54 year old elementary teacher had median
earnings $1,796 greater than those for craftsmen of similar age.[23]
The 25-34 year old elementary teacher had a $468 advantage over
the operatives in 1960, but the 45-54 year old elementary teacher
had a $1,234 advantage. The advantage of the secondary teacher
was, of course, greater still.

---

[23]Several particular craft occupations had higher median earnings than teachers, but the category as a whole did not.

Table 3.7

SELECTED CHARACTERISTICS OF PROFESSIONAL AND TECHNICAL OCCUPATIONS WITH LOWER 1959 MEDIAN INCOMES THAN ELEMENTARY AND SECONDARY TEACHERS, FOR THE EXPERIENCED MALE LABOR FORCE: 1960

Occupation	Median income (dollars)	Median school years completed	Percent of workers female	Percent of male professional workers in occupation
Professional workers, total	6,778	16.3	38	100.0
Elementary teachers	5,310	17.0	86	3.2
Secondary teachers	5,966	17.2	47	6.0
Professional occupations with lower median incomes than secondary teachers:				
(1) Actors	5,640	14.1	37	0.2
(2) Athletes	5,394	12.5	8	0.1
(3) Draftsmen	5,794	12.9	6	4.5
(4) Photographers	5,692	12.6	12	1.0
(5) Social and welfare workers	5,481	16.6	63	0.8
(6) Sports instructors and officials	5,519	16.5	32	1.2
(7) Technicians--engineering and physical sciences except electronics	5,688	12.8	13	3.6

(8) Therapists and healers	5,591	16.4	54	0.4
(9) Elementary teachers	5,310	17.0	86	3.2
Subtotal				15.0
Professional occupations with lower median incomes than elementary teachers:				
(1) Clergymen	4,151	17.1	2	4.3
(2) Dancers and dancing teachers	3,483	12.5	79	0.1
(3) Dietitians and nutritionists	3,963	12.7	93	--
(4) Entertainers, n.e.c.	3,674	12.1	23	0.2
(5) Foresters and conservationists	4,873	12.8	3	0.7
(6) Librarians	4,592	16.7	86	0.3
(7) Musicians and music teachers	4,757	14.9	56	1.9
(8) Nurses	4,400	13.0	98	0.3
(9) Recreation and group workers	4,395	15.1	43	0.5
(10) Religious workers	3,241	16.3	62	0.5
(11) Surveyors	4,486	12.5	4	0.1
(12) Technicians, medical and dental	4,614	12.8	62	1.2
Subtotal				10.1

Source: 1960 Census of Population: Vol. I, Characteristics of the Population, Part 1, U.S. Summary, Table 201; Subject Report PC(2)-7A, Occupational Characteristics, Tables 9 and 25.

Table 3.8

MEDIAN 1959 DOLLAR EARNINGS OF THE MALE EXPERIENCED
CIVILIAN LABOR FORCE, BY OCCUPATION AND AGE:
1960

Occupation	Total, 14 years and over	Age				
		18-24	25-34	35-44	45-54	55-64
Elementary teachers	5,201[a]	2,964	4,938	5,835	5,931	5,613
Secondary teachers	5,827	3,304	5,130	6,492	6,961	6,883
Professional workers	6,622	3,110	6,020	7,756	7,854	7,487
Farmers and farm managers	2,174	1,468	2,766	2,814	2,381	1,930
Managers, officials, and proprietors, nonfarm	6,651	3,762	6,085	7,306	7,182	6,680
Clerical workers	4,787	2,661	4,898	5,436	5,369	5,132
Sales workers	4,983	2,404	5,489	6,280	5,855	5,111
Craftsmen and foremen	5,239	3,257	5,305	5,714	5,450	5,148
Operatives	4,302	2,675	4,470	4,902	4,697	4,413
Private household workers	1,058	734	1,263	1,851	1,895	1,731
Other service workers	3,323	1,516	3,597	4,251	3,786	3,435
Farm laborers and foremen	1,070	913	1,682	1,673	1,566	1,312
Nonfarm laborers	2,949	1,811	3,444	3,690	3,509	3,321
Total, male experienced civilian labor force	4,624	2,468	4,906	5,461	5,112	4,619

[a]Since a very high proportion of male elementary teachers are
beginning teachers, the overall median salary is probably not
comparable to medians in other occupational groups.

Source: U.S. Bureau of the Census, 1960 Census of Population:
Subject Report PC(2)-7A, Occupational Characteristics, Tables 29
and 31.

All this suggests that teaching, as an occupation for men, will appeal most to those of lower-middle-class and working-class backgrounds. As far as economic rewards are concerned, teaching certainly compares very unfavorably to many, if not most, professional and managerial occupations, and there is little to indicate that the prestige awarded elementary and secondary teaching in our society compensates for the lower economic rewards. There is, moreover, some concrete evidence that teaching appeals more to men of lower-middle-class and working-class backgrounds than to men of upper-middle-class origins. In a 1956-1957 study of beginning teachers, Ward Mason found, first of all, that a higher proportion of the male than the female teachers came from blue-collar homes, and second, that the beginning teachers as a group were more likely to have come from blue-collar backgrounds than several other beginning professionals--e.g., medical students, independent attorneys, dental students, etc.[24] Thus, while Lazarsfeld and Thielens's study of college faculty in the social sciences indicated that about 15 percent of their sample had fathers who were blue-collar workers, and More's study of dental students indicated that 24 percent of them had blue-collar workers as fathers, Mason's study found that 36 percent of the beginning teachers as a whole had fathers in this occupational category.[25]

Future Sex Composition of the Profession. In light of the present discussion, the question which naturally arises is: What will happen to the sex composition of the elementary teaching profession? There are several factors indicating that men will become a more important numerical component of the profession. One indicator is that the sex composition of the profession has already begun to change. There are several reasons why this trend will probably continue for at least a while.

First and foremost, the United States has, in recent years, experienced an acute teacher shortage. This is in part

---

[24]Ward S. Mason, *The Beginning Teacher* (U.S. Department of Health, Education and Welfare, Circular No. 664, OE-23009), p. 13. Mason's figures for the other occupational groups came from various studies.

[25]*Ibid.* Mason's sources: Paul F. Lazarsfeld and Wagner Thielens, Jr., *The Academic Mind* (Glencoe: The Free Press, 1958), p. 401; Douglas M. More, "A Note on Occupational Origins of Health Service Professions," *American Sociological Review,* 25 (June 1960), p. 404.

the combined effect of the high postwar fertility and the low
Depression fertility. As a consequence, the ratio of adults to
children of elementary school age has declined markedly (Table
3.9). Furthermore, as Table 3.9 shows, there is little hope
that within the next twenty-five years or so this situation will
ease.[26] Bringing men into the profession is one way to try to
combat this shortage.

Table 3.9

ADULTS 20-64 YEARS OLD AND CHILDREN 5-14 YEARS OLD IN THE
POPULATION OF THE UNITED STATES:
1940-2000

Year	Percent of population		Ratio of adults to children
	5-14 years old	20-64 years old	
1940	17.0	58.7	3.45
1950	16.2	57.9	3.57
1960	19.8	52.5	2.65
1970[a]	19.8	51.3	2.59
1980	19.3	51.2	2.65
1985	20.1	50.7	2.52
1990	20.4	50.3	2.46
2000	19.6	51.9	2.65

[a]The estimates for 1970 to 2000 were, where relevant, the
Series B estimates--these assumed a moderately high fertility,
presuming only a moderate drop from the levels of fertility in
the last decade.

Sources: U.S. Bureau of the Census, 1960 Census of Population:
Vol. I, Characteristics of the Population, Part 1, U.S. Summary,
Table 47; Current Population Reports, Series P-25, No. 286,
Tables 4 and 8.

[26]The lack of increase in the projected proportion of the population in the major working years--20-64--is primarily because
the pinch in the pyramid caused by the Depression cohorts offsets
the expansion caused by the postwar fertility rise.

In addition to the problems posed by demographically induced teacher shortages, there are several others. Women tend to have a very intermittent labor force involvement, indicating that their commitment to work is not lifelong. There is a very high attrition rate of female teachers due to marriage, and childbearing and rearing. This results in a shortage of teachers experienced enough to be school administrators. Teacher shortages, then, affect two occupations--teaching and school administration. Men, on the other hand, usually of necessity have a lifelong commitment to the labor force. They therefore form a more stable teaching work force. This is especially important when it is necessary to fill administrative positions which may take a considerable amount of experience, and in which a certain continuity is highly desirable.

Another reason why there will probably continue to be an influx of males into the profession is the growing trend toward mass higher education, and the accommodation of our universities to this phenomenon. As higher education becomes more widespread, young men can increasingly be expected to go into teaching. With the greater proportion of youth going on to college, there will be an increasing number of men who will have achieved a higher education, but who will not be able to compete in the more demanding and difficult professions, and will fall back on teaching as a second or third choice.[27]

Finally, it is sometimes argued that there will be a continued change in the sex composition of the profession because there should be such a change. The reasoning behind this argument is that it would be healthier if children had some more direct experience with adult males--especially boys who may otherwise be somewhat lacking in acceptable adult male images.

There are thus several reasons why it is argued that the teaching profession will and should (and perhaps will because it should) become more evenly divided between the sexes. There are, however, several important factors which suggest that the change in the profession's sex composition will probably have its limitations. Perhaps the most important factor concerns the extent to which

---

[27]That education tends to attract the less gifted student is indicated from results of draft-deferment tests. Of 97,800 college freshmen who took the tests in the early 1950's, 53 percent passed. The proportion of engineering students who passed was 68 percent, 64 percent of the physical science and mathematics students, 59 percent of the students in the biological sciences, 57 percent of those in the social sciences--all above the average. Humanities students were a little below the average (52 percent passed), but only 27 percent of the education majors passed. Results for upperclassmen were similar. (Reported in Bestor, p. 209.)

the attraction of men to the teaching profession can solve the teaching shortage problem resulting from fertility changes and from the in-and-out labor force behavior characteristic of women teachers. While it is true that the labor force commitment of men, as opposed to women, tends to approximate a continuous 30-40 years, there is some evidence that the commitment of most male teachers to teaching is not very much greater than that of women. If this is true, then the recruitment of men to teaching will not help to alleviate the teaching shortage much more than the recruitment of additional women.

Ward Mason seems to have reached this conclusion in his Office of Education study of 7,150 beginning teachers (somewhat less than 10 percent of all beginning teachers in 1956-1957). His conclusion was that the "proportion of teachers with a really strong commitment to a continuous teaching career appears to be quite small...."[28] This statement was based on answers to a question on career plans (Table 3.10). Mason found that only 16 percent of the women beginning teachers planned to teach until retirement. A considerably higher proportion of the men planned to teach until retirement (29 percent), but this is still a very small percentage of all male beginning teachers. Nineteen percent of the male teachers planned to leave education for another occupation entirely, and 51 percent planned to go into a non-teaching job in education. For male elementary teachers, this percentage was even higher--60 percent of them planned to go into nonteaching jobs in education. Thus 71 percent of all the male teachers--74 percent of the male elementary teachers--did not plan to teach until retirement. As Mason remarks, "Men seem to see teaching primarily as a stepping-stone to some other type of occupation, either in or out of education."[29]

If these men realize their plans, it appears that while they might solve the problem of a shortage in school administrators, they will not provide a labor force that is much more committed to teaching on a lifetime basis than women. One might even argue that though 26 percent of the male elementary teachers, as opposed to 17 percent of the women, plan to teach until retirement, this overestimates the greater teaching "mileage" which can be expected from the men. This is because a departure of a man from teaching--either into school administration or a non-education occupation--is likely to be permanent. However, many women who retire from teaching in order to marry and raise a family may return to teaching at some later date. Thus 58 percent of the women beginning teachers in Mason's study said that

---

[28]Mason, p. 103.

[29]Ibid.

Table 3.10

CAREER PLANS OF BEGINNING TEACHERS, BY SEX AND TEACHING LEVEL:
1956-1957

(In percentages)

Career plans	Male teachers			Female teachers		
	Total	Elementary	Secondary	Total	Elementary	Secondary
Total with education plans	80	86	78	82	84	77
Teach until retirement	29	26	30	16	17	12
Nonteaching job in education	51	60	48	9	9	8
Homemaker, would want to return	--	--	--	58	58	57
Total with noneducation plans	19	14	22	18	16	23
Homemaker, would not want to return	--	--	--	12	12	15
Another occupation (including other noneducation plans as well)	19	14	22	6	4	9

Source: Ward S. Mason, The Beginning Teacher, U.S. Department of Health, Education and Welfare, Circular No. 644, OE-23009, Washington, 1961, Table 41.

they planned to be homemakers but wanted to return to teaching later (Table 3.10). In sum, if beginning male teachers achieve their occupational aims, it does not seem likely that there will be much of an accumulation of men in teaching. They, as well as women, are birds of passage as far as teaching is concerned.

It is important to realize that the greater the number of men in teaching the more unrealistic is the view that they can use teaching as a stepping-stone to administrative positions in education. There are, presumably, a limited number of administrative positions available at any given time, and the greater

the number of men in the occupation, the smaller are the chances
for each to achieve such a position. Thus we have the rather
paradoxical situation that teaching can be counted on to provide
career opportunities for men only so long as it remains a predominantly female occupation. For this reason, unless the rewards
offered to teachers per se are greatly improved relative to other
professional or managerial occupations, or unless the opportunities in these latter occupations decline, the trend toward a
growing number of men in the profession may very well cease. The
trend may have lying within it, so to speak, the seeds of its own
destruction.[30] There is certainly in Mason's study ample evidence
that the beginning male teachers (but not the female teachers to
any significant degree) were dissatisfied with the economic rewards of the occupation. Less than half were satisfied with
their current salary, the time needed to reach peak salary (and
this is probably in some administrative post), or the maximum
salary possible. Furthermore, even though a substantial component
of these teachers had lower-middle-class and working-class backgrounds, only 28 percent were satisfied with their "salary compared to that of other occupations in [their] area open to people
with [their] level of education."[31]

It is easy to understand why teaching as a lifelong career
might initially but not permanently appeal to the upwardly mobile
young man. The economic advantages of teaching compared to those
in many blue-collar and clerical occupations might look fine to
such a young man when he is making the decision to go into teaching. But in the process of going to school for several years and
becoming a teacher, his associates change and his knowledge of
the world and its opportunities as well. Thus, his reference
group changes. Then the advantages of teaching seem to diminish.
He is less and less likely to compare himself to a welder, and
rather starts to compare himself to others with four years or
more of college. In this comparison his profession suffers, as
Mason's statistics on satisfaction indicate. Teaching then becomes a stepping-stone, if it has not been one all along.

---

[30]There is the possibility, of course, that many men who go into teaching are simply not of the caliber to go into more highly
rewarded occupations, so that the latter, in effect, do not compete for this source of labor. In that case, male teachers who
did not advance into administrative positions and who became dissatisfied with their lot might, of necessity, have to stay in
teaching. If this were the case, the implications are, to say the
least, somewhat disturbing, and would seem to militate against
policies promoting the extensive use of male teachers.

[31]Mason, p. 80. Between 75 and 98 percent of the male teachers
were satisfied with the 17 other items they were questioned about,
so the replies to the salary questions stand out.

If young men tend to regard teaching as a stepping-stone to bigger and better things, what are the chances that the relative economic position of teaching will be improved and hence more of its recruits retained? Even if some improvement in the relative economic position of teachers were to occur, it seems unlikely that teaching--particularly elementary teaching--will achieve economic returns comparable to many other managerial and professional occupations. For one thing, the gap is too large. Second, as Caplow has pointed out, occupations with a large proportion of female workers tend to be vulnerable, since it is almost impossible for a woman's occupation to be effectively monopolized by the incumbents. It is thus difficult to force the price of labor up in such occupations,[32] though the recent militancy of teachers' unions indicates that some improvements are on the way. In general, low wages have been characteristic of the history of teaching in the United States. School districts, for practical and economic reasons, have for over a hundred years typically shown themselves willing to hire cheaper female labor. This is how women got their start in the profession in the first place. It seems unlikely, therefore, that male teachers will in the future displace female elementary teachers. Rather, they will be used to supplement the female teaching force, and to fill the administrative positions in which women seem to have little interest--at least as indicated by their career plans (Table 3.10). As long as women form a significant proportion of the profession, it will probably be most difficult to drive up the price of their labor so that it will be comparable to that in other professional occupations. And unless the earnings of teachers go up tremendously, it is unlikely that very many men will either enter the occupation or stay there.

Summary. In this brief review of some of the problems of the teaching profession, there are several points I have been trying to emphasize. First of all, women provided a very attractive combination of characteristics in the beginnings of public school teaching in the United States--availability when suitable male labor was scarce, some education, and cheapness. However, the continued use of women in teaching, plus the rapid industrialization of the United States, has had several consequences critical to the nature of the teaching profession. Industrialization has led to a much greater need for a generally educated and specifically trained labor force. On the one hand, this has entailed a growing emphasis on finishing high school and going on to college. This means that for the same population more teachers are

---

[32]Caplow, p. 236.

required. On the other hand, it has entailed a rise in the educational requirements for teachers. If a child is expected to
learn not only the "three R's," but many other subjects as well,
his teacher must be more extensively educated. Thus, the amount
of preparation desired and required of teachers has been steadily
increasing. This has been enhanced and sometimes subverted as
well, by the pressure to raise training requirements in order to
increase the prestige of the occupation. The continued utilization
of women has meant that workers with such training could be acquired cheaply, and that teaching did not have to compete with
more remunerative occupations requiring a fairly lengthy training
program. As a result, teaching has developed by and large into
an occupation which is economically noncompetitive with occupations requiring the same number of years in school--though not
necessarily the same difficulty in the course of instruction.

As previously noted, the major appeal of elementary teaching to men is, first of all, probably to males of working-class
and lower-middle-class backgrounds who have mobility aspirations.
The rewards of teaching, particularly if the ultimate goal is
administration, compare favorably to those in many, though by no
means all, blue-collar and lower white-collar occupations. Second, elementary teaching probably appeals to young men without
either the ability, motivation, or quality of education to compete in the more difficult professions. The increasingly mass
character of higher education provides many young men such as
these with the opportunity to enter teaching. Even so, since the
opportunities for administrative positions in education are necessarily limited, there will probably be a limit to the extent to
which the male elementary teaching force will expand, and elementary teaching will remain a predominantly female occupation.

So far, our discussion has revealed a few of the factors
making for stability in the sex composition of elementary teaching,
and a few which tend to promote changes in sex composition. Next,
we shall consider how these and several additional factors operate in other occupations.

Factors Promoting the Development and Persistence of Sex-Labeled Jobs

Labor Costs and Labor Availability.[33] We have seen that
the availability of cheap female labor was probably a very important factor in the widespread use of women in elementary school-

---

[33]For my analysis of these and other factors promoting the sex
labeling of jobs, I am greatly indebted to the discussion in
Womanpower, pp. 220-244 and 86-109.

teaching. This combination of characteristics--cheapness plus availability--has usually been fairly typical of female labor in the United States, and has promoted the use of women in many jobs.[34] For this reason, as well as others, certain occupations have been almost monopolized by women, and there has been little motivation on the part of employers to try to switch to male labor or for men to enter the occupation.

The combination of cheapness and availability seems to have been a major factor in the utilization of women in semi-skilled factory work. Edith Abbott, for example, argues this in her discussion of the establishment of the factory system in the United States at the end of the eighteenth century and the beginning of the nineteenth century.[35] She points out that

> the ease with which any man could become a freeholder and the superior chances of success in agriculture made it difficult to find men who were willing to work in manufacturing establishments....Moreover, as a question of national economy, fear was expressed regarding the possible injury to our agricultural interests if much labor were diverted from the land. Manufactures, if they were to be established, must not, it was emphatically said, be built at the expense of agriculture.[36]

She goes on to say that the United States did not have many employed in the cotton industry before the introduction of the factory system--at least many men. As a consequence, "the establishment of the factory system...substantially meant, with us, the creation of new work, and made imperative a large increase in our wage-earning population."[37] While men did not seem eager to leave the land to enter factory work--at least for the wages being offered--the need for women on the farm was much less, and they supplied a ready and willing labor source.[38] This was particularly

---

[34]The cheapness of women, compared to men, is quite well documented. For the nineteenth and early twentieth centuries, see Abbott, pp. 305-14, and Stanley Lebergott, Manpower in Economic Growth (New York: McGraw-Hill Book Co., 1964), pp. 126-27; for the present-day differentials, see Women's Bureau, Economic Indicators Relating to Equal Pay, Pamphlet 9 (Washington: U.S. Government Printing Office, 1963), pp. 5ff.

[35]Abbott, Ch. 4, "Establishment of the Factory System," pp. 48-62.

[36]P. 48.

[37]P. 49.

[38]Ibid., pp. 55ff. See also Lebergott, pp. 125ff.

true of farmers' daughters, for whom the possibilities of gainful employment were rather limited at the beginning of the nineteenth century. For these reasons, and for others as well, women formed a major source of labor in the cotton industry from its very earliest days. The cotton industry, in turn, has been a major source of operatives jobs for American women.[39]

This combination of cheapness plus availability was not, of course, typical of female labor alone. To some extent, children also provided a ready source of cheap labor. However, aside from native women, immigrants--both male and female--provided the most important source of cheap labor for developing industries. In some cases, immigrant labor filled jobs considered inappropriate for native labor--heavy manual work such as canal and railroad building, which cheap native female labor could not engage in, and domestic service, in which native white women were reluctant to engage. At times, immigrant labor even successfully competed with cheap native female labor.[40] But however important immigrant labor became in the latter half of the nineteenth century, and on into the twentieth century, immigration was still quite modest when the cotton industry was first developing in the early nineteenth century, and native women and children provided the main source of cheap, noncommitted labor.[41] In time, of course, immigrant labor--both male and female--replaced native labor in the New England cotton mills.[42]

Skilled Cheap Labor. It is undoubtedly true that women have always provided a cheap source of labor. But to draw from this the conclusion that a demand for female labor is simply a demand for cheap labor rather glibly ignores several facets of the situation. It has not been the cheapness of female labor alone which has been decisive in its general use in certain jobs,

---

[39] In 1900, for example, about 22 percent of all female operatives were in textiles and knitting, and in 1940, 19 percent; however, by 1960 the proportion was down to about 7 percent (Kaplan and Casey, Tables 6 and 6b; 1960 Census, Characteristics, Table 201).

[40] See, for example, Abbott, p. 228.

[41] In 1820, for example, only 8,385 migrated to the United States; in 1830, 23,322. Migrations in the 100,000's became standard only after the 1840's (U.S. Bureau of the Census, Historical Statistics of the United States, Colonial Times to 1957, p. 57).

[42] See Abbott, Ch. VII, "Early Mill Operatives: Conditions of Life and Work," pp. 109-147.

but rather its cheapness in combination with other characteristics. One of these combinations is cheapness plus skill.

General or specific skills, in combination with cheapness, have been important factors in the utilization of women in several areas aside from teaching. There are many other jobs in which women predominate today which, like elementary teaching, offer relatively low economic rewards, but nevertheless require a fair amount of education. This is illustrated in Table 3.11, which shows income and educational information for those occupations that are at least 51 percent female and in which the median years of school completed is greater than 11.1--the median for the total male experienced civilian labor force. What we see is that, relative to the educational attainment of the average male worker, the average number of school years completed is higher--for male as well as female workers--in several predominantly female occupations. Yet in most cases the average 1959 income of workers in these occupations does not compare favorably with the median income for all male workers. In other words, the more educated labor in several "female" occupations is not rewarded by a proportionately higher income. These occupations account for quite a sizable proportion of female workers: 71 percent of all women in the professional and technical category, and 98 percent of those in clerical occupations--a total of about 42 percent of all female workers.

There is evidence, furthermore, that the educational achievement typical of women in several white-collar occupations is not a purely gratuitous accompaniment of employing female labor, but is itself a characteristic much in demand. Even twenty-five years ago, Noland and Bakke found, for example, that over 90 percent of the employers in both New Haven and Charlotte preferred clerical workers to have a high-school education or better.[43]

In general, it seems that in the course of American history, the need for cheap but educated labor tended to promote reliance on women in certain occupations. The continuously growing demand in an industrializing society for workers with a fairly high level of general education plus some special skills has (except perhaps in periods of depression) resulted in a chronic shortage of "middle quality" labor. The shortage of this kind of labor has never been successfully alleviated by immigration, an important source of relatively unskilled labor. In such a situation, it is bound to be true that some occupations--secretarial work, for example--are less successful than others

---

[43] E.W. Noland and E.W. Bakke, Workers Wanted: A Study of Employers' Hiring Policies, Preferences, and Practices in New Haven and Charlotte (New York: Harper & Bros., 1949), pp. 194-195.

Table 3.11

RELATIVE INCOME AND EDUCATIONAL STANDING OF SELECTED OCCUPATIONS: 1960[a]

Occupation	Ratio of median number of school years completed in occupation to median for total male labor force[b]		Ratio of median income in occupation to median for total male labor force[c]	
	Male	Female	Male	Female
TOTAL	1.00	1.09	1.00	0.59
Professional workers				
Dancers and dancing teachers	1.12	1.12	0.83	0.61
Dietitians and nutritionists	1.14	1.19	0.76	0.68
Librarians	1.50	1.46	1.01	0.77
Musicians and music teachers	1.34	1.33	1.03	0.29
Nurses	1.17	1.19	0.84	0.71
Recreation and group workers	1.36	1.32	1.00	0.78
Social and welfare workers	1.49	1.48	1.04	0.87
Religious workers	1.47	1.21	0.77	0.49
Elementary teachers	1.53	1.48	1.03	0.85
Teachers, n.e.c.	1.48	1.45	1.10	0.74
Therapists and healers	1.48	1.45	0.97	0.83

Clerical workers			
Library attendants and assistants	1.23	1.18	0.55	0.54
Physicians' and dentists' office attendants	1.12	1.12	0.68	0.53
Bank tellers	1.14	1.12	0.84	0.63
Bookkeepers	1.14	1.12	0.89	0.64
File clerks	1.12	1.10	0.75	0.59
Office-machine operators	1.13	1.12	0.96	0.68
Payroll and timekeeping clerks	1.13	1.12	1.00	0.73
Receptionists	1.13	1.13	0.77	0.57
Secretaries	1.15	1.14	1.05	0.71
Stenographers	1.14	1.14	1.02	0.70
Typists	1.13	1.13	0.80	0.64
Telephone operators	1.11	1.10	1.07	0.67
Cashiers	1.08	1.08	0.78	0.53
Clerical workers, n.e.c.	1.12	1.12	0.99	0.66
Sales workers			
Demonstrators	1.08	1.09	--[d]	0.50
Hucksters and peddlers	0.92	1.09	0.82	0.16

[a] Includes occupations in which at least 51 percent of the workers were female and where the median school years completed was greater than 11.1--the median for the total male experienced civilian labor force.

[b] Experienced civilian labor force.

[c] Wage and salary workers in the experienced civilian labor force who worked 50-52 weeks in 1959.

[d] Base not large enough to compute a median.

Source: U.S. Bureau of the Census, 1960 Census of Population: Subject Report PC(2)-7A, Occupational Characteristics, Tables 9 and 28.

in competing for middle-quality labor. It is the occupations in
a poorer position to compete for such labor that tend to utilize
female labor. Once recourse has been made to female labor to
provide quality labor at a low price, employers tend to get used
to relatively well-educated workers (standards have been going
up, not down) who have been working for much less than men who
have received a comparable education. To substitute men to any
considerable extent would require either a rise in the price paid
for labor or a decline in the quality of the labor, or both.[44]
Unless there are some very compelling reasons for it, it seems
unlikely that many female occupations of this type will radically
change their sex composition.

Sex-linked Characteristics. In addition to the advantage
of cheapness, another reason women were extensively used in early
American manufacturing was that the young industries could bene-
fit from the utilization of skills learned by women as part of
their female role. Two of the major early industries were the
cotton and clothing industries, both engaged in producing goods
women had traditionally been involved in producing in the home.
In the case of cotton, women had frequently had some experience
in spinning and weaving before they entered the mill, and hence
were already somewhat familiar with the tasks they were to carry
out there.[45] In the clothing industry, prior to the invention of
the sewing machine in 1850, all garments had to be hand-sewn.
Given that fact, the advantages of using women are obvious. Nor
did the introduction of the sewing machine greatly affect the
major reliance on women.[46] The development of the cotton and
clothing industries in the United States suggests, therefore,
that one reason employers may demand either male or female labor
exclusively is because they desire workers with traits that are
considered attributes of one sex or the other. Skill in spinning,
weaving, and sewing are traditionally skills associated with the
female role. Many other cases can be cited of sex-linked characteristics promoting, at some point in an occupation's history,
the almost exclusive use of either men or women. These characteristics may be innate or acquired--it matters little, for our
purposes, which they are. Furthermore, they may not even be
proven traits of one sex or the other--it is sufficient that employers believe they are, or believe that one sex has an advantage over the other in some important respect.

---

[44]Since the civil rights act of 1964 prohibits discrimination
in pay rates on the basis of sex, a rise in salary would presumably have to be offered to women as well as men in order to
attract more males into the occupation.

[45]Abbott, pp. 91ff.

[46]Ibid., Ch. X, "The Clothing Industry," pp. 215-245.

There have been several jobs in American society--particularly in the past--which have required a fair amount of physical strength. Women have not been considered suitable for such work, so jobs requiring much physical strength have tended automatically to be labeled male.[47] Noland and Bakke found, for example, in their 1940's study of hiring practices in New Haven and Charlotte, that about 90 percent of employers preferred men for common laboring jobs--those in which physical strength is most likely to be needed--and about 75 percent **required** men; women were preferred only for cleaning jobs.[48]

Women are supposed by many employers to have greater manual dexterity than men. This may or may not be true, but that is not particularly important. What is important is the extent to which employers believe it, and let this belief guide their hiring policies. For example, in a study of job opportunities for female technicians, the Women's Bureau found that "firms manufacturing small delicate electronic units emphasize the importance of finger dexterity and patience in making precise measurements with small instruments and usually consider women better qualified than men for such jobs."[49] As this quote indicates, women are also frequently credited with a greater patience with routine tasks than men. Noland and Bakke found, for example, that employers in New Haven and Charlotte felt that, with regard to production workers, women are "less likely to be dissatisfied with jobs which are repetitive or monotonous and for which pay is relatively low."[50]

---

[47] Twelve states, for example, have statutes, rules, regulations, or wage orders which specify the maximum weight women employees are allowed to lift, carry, or lift and carry. The maximum weights vary from 15 to 35 pounds (U.S. Women's Bureau, _1962 Handbook on Women Workers_, Bulletin No. 285 [Washington, 1963], p. 146). Also see the discussion in _Womanpower_, pp. 226-227 and 95-96.

[48] Noland and Bakke, pp. 184-185. In a study of job opportunities for women as technicians, the Women's Bureau found that in the electronics field, for example, "firms producing large electronic units often require their technicians to lift and move heavy equipment; they may, therefore, refuse to hire a woman for such work if they think it is beyond her strength" (_Careers for Women as Technicians_, Women's Bureau Bulletin 282 [Washington, 1962], p. 3).

[49] _Ibid._, p. 3. This belief also cropped up several times in employers conferences conducted by the National Manpower Council. See, for example, _Womanpower_, p. 93.

[50] Noland and Bakke, pp. 25-26.

This was also a factor, they found, in women being preferred over men in clerical positions.[51]

Finally, sheer feminine (and masculine too, I presume) appeal is considered an important factor at times. For example, in the 1960 NOMA study (see footnote 51), about 28 percent of the companies surveyed indicated sex appeal was a requirement for some office jobs, and that it is given serious consideration in the employment of workers for jobs such as receptionist, switchboard operator, secretary, and stenographer.[52]

Pre-job Training. A major disadvantage in the employment of women is that their labor force participation tends to be intermittent. The employer is thus faced with the possibility that he will spend a considerable amount of time and money training someone who will retire from work altogether. For this reason, jobs requiring a considerable amount of on-the-job training entail a certain risk for the employer, which he understandably wishes to minimize. On the other hand, any job requiring relatively little on-the-job training is, as such, favorable to the employment of women, and it has sometimes been feared that women would largely replace men in semiskilled work--an eventuality which does not appear to be taking place. This view overlooks some of the more important facets of the situation. It is not that jobs favorable to the employment of women require no skills, but that the skills required can be obtained before employment takes place. This was one important advantage to the utilization of women in the cotton mills--often they had already acquired a certain facility in spinning and weaving before they were recruited into the factories. The trend in general education and training in specific skills is such that it is very frequently the community at large and the individual workers themselves who pay for their education and training. The employer, then, receives workers whose training he did not have to pay for.

Over the long run, female workers have been turning increasingly to white-collar occupations--occupations that frequently require a fairly high general level of education, as well as some specialized training. But it is an education and training

---

[51]Ibid., p. 65. In a 1960 survey of almost 2,000 business, industrial, and service organizations in the United States and Canada, the National Office Management Association found that one reason employers preferred women over men in some clerical jobs was the belief that women were more patient (Charles E. Ginder, "Factor of Sex in Office Employment," Office Executive, 36 [February 1961], p. 10). See also Womanpower, p. 104.

[52]Ginder, p. 11.

that the woman brings with her to the job, not which she acquires on the job--though of course most workers will perform better with experience. Occupations such as secretary, schoolteacher, librarian, nurse, and the many types of laboratory technicians are examples of occupations for which a fair amount of education and some specific training are required; however, the special training required is not so rigorous that it is not worthwhile for women to acquire it. The main point is that though these are occupations which require skills, they do not require long-term commitments on the part of employees and can be almost entirely trained for before working, making women less costly risks as workers.

Tradition. Another very important factor operating to put a sex label on jobs, and more frequently to keep the sex label there, is tradition. In the nineteenth century, for example, a high proportion of female workers were engaged in "female occupations" which were female occupations not just because female labor was cheap, but also because they had traditionally been female occupations. They remained so despite changes in the place of work and the means of production. Thus, as we have already noted, women had always been the spinners at home and, to some extent, the weavers too, and this work was assigned to them in the mills. Women had made the family's clothes at home, and continued to do so in the factory. They had nursed the sick at home, and took up that occupation outside the home in the hospitals. They took care of their own and other people's houses as domestics. Even today, a very high proportion of all women operatives are engaged in occupations that have traditionally been feminine in the sense that we have just been discussing.

Regardless of the reason women or men were initially used in a job, tradition tends to make a particular sex label stick. In other words, each time a job becomes vacant, the question of whether a man or a woman is to be hired is not up for debate. Rather the job is usually considered a woman's or a man's job and, unless some difficulty is encountered, so it will remain. For example, in the Women's Bureau study of technicians, to which we have already referred, it was found that an electronics firm in which the technicians work with very small units declared that women would be very readily hired if they were qualified but no women had ever applied for such a job.

The obstacle of traditional thinking appears to affect some employers as well as some women. A representative of one State employment office reported to the Women's Bureau that employers in the local area almost always specified men on their job orders for technicians. However, placement officers at that office noted that employers seemed to be willing to

105

hire women when they were referred. It had apparently not occurred to some employers that women might be
available for such work.[53]

The National Manpower Council strongly emphasizes the
importance of tradition in its discussion of the seven employer
conferences it undertook in the womanpower study.[54]

Many employers reported that the hiring of women is
frequently governed by traditional attitudes which
establish what jobs are suitable for them. These
traditional attitudes, it was emphasized, are operative among workers, as well as at the management
level. The distinctions between "men's" and "women's"
jobs appear to be particularly sharp in certain manufacturing fields; and in professional, service, and
sales work, jobs are often closed to women because
it is taken for granted that they should be held by
men. It is believed that, if women are placed in
such jobs, they are likely to produce negative re-
actions not only among male supervisors, fellow employees, and customers, but also in the public at
large.[55]

The study goes on to point out that

conferees from various manufacturing concerns re-
peatedly offered examples of occupational fields in
which there has been a comparatively rigid, and often
arbitrarily determined, division of jobs within a
plant, a company, or an industry. In many cases
these jobs are considered the exclusive preserve of
either men or women out of traditional practice,
without any apparent basis in present social attitudes, employee characteristics and competence, or
labor costs. In some cases, these considerations
originally did operate to determine job assignments,
and though they may no longer apply, the traditional
divisions continue. The fact that a particular job
has customarily been performed by a man or by a woman may exert a stronger influence than any other in

---

[53] _Careers for Women as Technicians_, p. 8.

[54] _Womanpower_, Ch. III, "Women in Business and Industry: An
Employer Appraisal," pp. 86-109.

[55] _Ibid._, pp. 88-89.

determining to whom the job will be assigned when a
replacement is made.[56]

The inertia and security of tradition therefore greatly help
maintain a status quo in the sex labeling of jobs, regardless of
whether any rational reason for the label still exists. Provided
the job does not change greatly, and the usual source of labor
does not change its characteristics or become less abundant, there
is little reason why employers would be motivated to switch sexes.

Mixed Work Groups and Women Supervisors. Two related
factors which tend to keep the sex composition of a job homogeneous are the difficulties involved in having work groups made
up of both men and women, and the problems--real or presumed--
involved with having women in supervisory positions.[57] As Caplow
argues, both sexes have been trained from youth not to compete,
and this presents problems when male and female workers are on
equal job levels.[58] In addition, if one or two women are introduced into a male work group, "the necessary adaptations to her
presence appear excessive to everyone concerned, including im-
mediate changes in verbal habits, dress and comportment, and
potential changes in the organization of the group."[59] If so
many women are introduced that the sex ratio is almost even,
then the sexes will tend to form two groups which may be quite
hostile to each other.[60] Furthermore, employers may have trouble
interesting men in jobs staffed predominantly by women unless it
is obvious that the man is in some ways a privileged worker, one
with "great expectations," such as in teaching, for example. The
National Manpower Council found, in this regard, that "especially
in factories...men will avoid jobs they regard as 'women's.'
These are usually the jobs in which a high proportion of the
workers, generally over 60 percent, are women."[61]

If mixed work groups were common--that is, if men and women
were used interchangeably in jobs and in full competition with

---

[56]P. 89.

[57]For a general discussion of these, see Caplow, pp. 237ff.
[Paperback edition.]

[58]Ibid., p. 243.

[59]Ibid., p. 242.

[60]Ibid.

[61]These findings are from the results of the seven employers
conferences held by the National Manpower Council (Womanpower,
pp. 90-91).

each other--one obvious result would be the entry of women into
supervisory positions more often than is now the case. However,
in addition to any other factors which may militate against it,
there appears to be a fairly widespread belief that it is best
not to have women as supervisors. In the Noland and Bakke study
in the 1940's, for example, 74 percent of the New Haven employers
and 83 percent of the employers in Charlotte preferred men for
administrative and executive positions.[62] One of the major reasons given was that they thought men should deal with men--i.e.,
most clients, other management people, suppliers, etc., were
male, and it was not appropriate to have women dealing with them.
Another major reason cited was that men supervisors commanded
more respect, even from women.[63] Similarly, the National Manpower
Council found in their 1950's study that most of the employers
with whom they came in contact "maintained that women as well as
men generally prefer male supervisors. It was asserted that wom-
en are more likely to accept instructions from a man than from a
woman...."[64] The 1960 study conducted by the NOMA also indicated
that men were somewhat more favored than women as supervisors--
68 percent of the responding firms said that male supervisors had
a better chance for success in supervising an all-female department, as opposed to 11 percent who favored female supervisors,
and 21 percent who had no opinion on the subject. In addition,
65 percent said that they had qualms about placing a woman super-
visor over a department which employs male workers.[65]

As far as more sociological analyses of this problem are
concerned, Whyte's study is probably one of the few that deals
with it. He argues that frictions tend to arise in an organization
when lower-status individuals try to originate action for those of
higher status. He points out that "in our society most men grow
up to be comfortable in a relationship in which they originate for
women, and to be uneasy, if not more seriously disturbed, when the
originations go in the other direction."[66]

---

[62]Noland and Bakke, pp. 184-185.

[63]Ibid., pp. 79-80. The hesitancy to deal with women carries
over into professional work. See, for example, Josephine Williams,
"Patients and Prejudice: Lay Attitudes Toward Women Physicians,"
American Journal of Sociology, 51 (January 1946), pp. 283-287.

[64]Womanpower, p. 106.

[65]Ginder, p. 13.

[66]William F. Whyte, "The Social Structure of the Restaurant,"
American Journal of Sociology, LIV (January 1949), p. 305. See
also Caplow's discussion of his thesis that it is considered dis-
graceful for a man to be directly subordinated to a woman (pp. 238f.

Whyte uses the various relationships between men and women in a restaurant as a prime example of this thesis. He observed that in several complementary roles--waitress-counterman and waitress-barman, for example--men seemed to resent getting orders from women, and all sorts of devices were utilized which, regardless of their original intent, had the function of insulating the man from the waitress, so that she could not directly give him orders.[67] To my knowledge, Whyte's thesis has not received any further empirical test. Nevertheless, whether or not problems usually arise when women initiate action for men or whether or not women make effective supervisors, employers and workers alike frequently seem to believe that women supervisors are not as effective as men. To the extent this belief guides hiring and promotion policies, supervisory and executive jobs will tend to be reserved for men.

Our discussion so far has stressed factors which promote the attachment of female as much as, if not more than, male sex labels to jobs. Let us now consider three important factors which tend to make and keep many jobs predominantly male.[68]

Career Continuity. A key factor affecting the utilization of women in certain jobs is the extent to which career continuity is important. Career continuity may be important for a number of reasons--to acquire skills, to maintain already acquired skills, or to establish seniority and prove one's loyalty to an organization. We may distinguish at least two types of career continuity. First, it may be essential for an individual to be continuously employed in one firm for a number of years before some jobs are available to him. Many bureaucratic systems stress this sort of continuity, mainly for the reasons outlined above-- the individual has to get to know the organization before he can be of use to it in certain jobs for which training within the organization is necessary, and he must establish his loyalty by being around for an extended period. Many executive positions seem to require career continuity of this sort. In a 1952 study of executives, for example, Fortune magazine found that 60 percent of the executives had worked for no other or only one other company before joining their present company; 77 percent had worked for two other firms or less.[69] Continuity of employment

---

[67] Whyte, pp. 365ff.

[68] The following discussion relies heavily on Caplow's analysis in Sociology of Work, Ch. 10, "Occupations of Women," pp. 230-247.

[69] This study is based on information obtained by Fortune from the three highest paid men in the 250 biggest industrial

may also be very important in some manual work, where certain jobs in plants are given men on the basis of seniority or experience in several other jobs in the plant.

In cases where continuity of employment within one firm may not be essential, a second type of continuity--that of continuous involvement within an occupation or an industry--may be of great importance. This is certainly the case in many technical professions. Such professions as medicine and other scientific fields require continuity of involvement within the field in order to keep up skills and to keep abreast of a rapidly changing profession. Yet a certain amount of job shifting may be expected. So labor force continuity, but not necessarily continued involvement in one organization, may be essential. Continuity of employment within the field is important also in craft occupations with their institutionalized apprenticeship systems.

In general, as has been amply documented in Chapter 1, the occupational careers of women are usually not continuous. Their labor force participation is closely geared to the family life cycle. Although an increasing proportion of married women with young children do work, the proportion is still a small one, and labor force participation for most women is, on the whole, intermittent. To the extent that continuous involvement within an occupation or on a particular job is an important ingredient of success or a prerequisite to getting into certain jobs, women are obviously seriously handicapped.[70]

In addition to the handicaps which women with professional or managerial aspirations experience because of the intermittent nature of their employment, they are handicapped by certain attitudes among employers. Many women cannot get necessary on-the-job training or promotions because employers feel that it is not worth the risk--women cannot be depended upon to be around long enough to make training and promoting them pay off. Noland and Bakke found, for example, that one reason employers did not want to have women in executive positions was that "it is desirable that this group shall have as little turnover as possible. Too many women are likely to marry and leave the job."[71] The National Manpower Council also found that

---

companies on the basis of sales, 25 biggest railroads, and the 25 biggest utilities. See Editors of _Fortune,_ The Executive Life (Garden City, N.Y.: Doubleday & Co., 1956), p. 31. [Dolphin Books

[70]See _Womanpower,_ p. 105.

[71]Noland and Bakke, p. 80.

an employer will hesitate to make a significant training investment in a woman in order to qualify her for
promotion, if he thinks that she may withdraw from
paid employment for any one of a series of reasons
which lie outside the work situation. Considerations
of cost related to work continuity, rather than prej-
udicial attitudes against women as such, were said to
be particularly responsible for the reluctance to promote women to higher-level posts.[72]

Although women move in and out of the labor force more than men,
it is not certain that women, on the average, quit their jobs
more often than men do.[73] From the point of view of a return on
a training investment, it is, of course, job turnover which is
most significant. Nevertheless, employers seem to believe that
women can be depended upon less than men, and act accordingly.
It is probably true, however, that on the average men quit jobs
somewhat more often than women for reasons which are job-connected
and hence within the competitive realm of the market.

   Motivation. An important characteristic of female workers
is that they tend to be secondary breadwinners. As Caplow has
emphasized, this may result in wage discrimination.[74] There are
other important concomitants as well, however. One is that a
woman's commitment to work and to a career in an occupation may be
seriously weakened. A great deal usually depends on the success
of a man in the occupational world, and for this reason his commitment and aspirations are likely to be bound up heavily in his
work, even though the primary motivating force of his life might
be the welfare of his family. His familial and work commitments
pull together to a considerable degree. For women, on the other
hand, high occupational aspirations are not usually seen as promoting the welfare of the family, but rather as competing with it
for the woman's scarce resources of time, energy, and emotional
interest. As a consequence, women's occupational aspirations
are frequently low. They seldom want to rise from file clerks
to executives in companies--the work responsibilities become too
onerous. Nor do they want to go through training processes as
time-consuming and difficult as medicine, law, and the academic
professions require. It is simply not worthwhile for what most
women want to get out of work.

---

[72]Womanpower, p. 105. See also pp. 94-95.

[73]Womanpower cites data from several studies to show that female turnover rates are not uniformly higher than male turnover
rates. See pp. 241ff.

[74]Caplow, p. 235.

This lack of career goals is well demonstrated in two surveys of women college graduates. If any group had career goals, one would expect it to be these. In the first, the Women's Bureau of the Department of Labor in cooperation with the National Vocational Guidance Association surveyed June 1957 women college graduates during the following winter.[75] One of the questions was: "What are your plans for future employment?" Seven alternatives were listed on the questionnaire. These and the percent distribution of the responses are given in Table 3.12.

Table 3.12

CAREER PLANS OF JUNE 1957 WOMEN COLLEGE GRADUATES,
BY MARITAL STATUS

Career plans	Total	Single	Married	Other[a]
Total	100	100	100	100
Plan to have a career	18	19	14	52
Plan to work indefinitely but have no interest in a career	10	10	9	27
Plan to work only as necessary--for economic reasons	6	4	11	11
Plan to stop work when have children	40	33	54	1
Plan to work for a short time after marriage	18	25	6	3
Plan to stop work when marry	6	9	--	4
Do not plan to work in the foreseeable future	2	b	5	2
Other plans	b	b	b	--

[a]Widowed, separated, and divorced.

[b]Less than one percent.

Source: Women's Bureau, First Jobs of College Women, Bulletin No. 268 (Washington, 1959), pp. 41 and 44.

[75]U.S. Women's Bureau, First Jobs of College Women, Bulletin No. 268 (Washington, 1959).

The second survey, reported by Alice Rossi, consisted of a questionnaire sent to a sample of women college graduates three years beyond graduation. The women were asked: "An American woman can be very successful in a variety of ways. Which of the following would you most like to be yourself?" Rossi reports that the most frequent answers were: to be the mother of several accomplished children, and to be the wife of a prominent man.[76]

The career motivation of these women certainly does not appear pronounced. Now it may be true that most men, like most women, do not have high career ambitions--or, at least, the dedication, the willingness to compete and to take the risks and responsibilities that go along with achieving high occupational goals. Nevertheless, it is probably true that more men than women, few in number as both groups may be, are likely to have high aspirations and the characteristics that go with them. It is certainly true that the pressures of the male role (particularly for middle-class males) operate to reinforce high occupational aspirations, while the pressures of the female role conflict with such aspirations.

In the final analysis, however, whether or not female motivation, on the average, is very different from male, employers tend to believe that women have lower career aspirations than men, and they act accordingly in their hiring and promotion policies. The National Manpower Council, for example, reported that

> the attitudes of women toward work, it was said, often help determine the range of job opportunities open to them. Women were described as usually less willing than men to make sacrifices required to secure the training which would qualify them for advancement. Frequently, it was reported, they are even unwilling to take advantage of chances for immediate promotion. It was suggested that this lack of interest and initiative could be both a cause and an effect of women's restricted opportunities in the working world.[77]

Geographical Mobility. A final factor operating to keep women out of several occupations concerns their ability and/or willingness to migrate or not to migrate, as the case may be.

---

[76] Alice S. Rossi, "Women in Science: Why So Few?" Science, 148 (May 1965), p. 1198. This article is, in general, an excellent discussion of present incompatibilities between marriage and professional careers for upper-middle-class women.

[77] Womanpower, p. 94. See also pp. 104ff.

Many professional and managerial careers require a certain amount of geographical mobility--from one company location to another or from one job to another. A married woman is seriously handicapped in this respect. Her husband's career usually has priority, and if it is advantageous for him to move across the country, his wife may have to leave a good job without any job, much less a good one, in sight at their destination. Or it may be necessary for the husband to stay put, while the career opportunities for his wife would be greatly enhanced if they could move. Thus, in general, the national and sometimes international travel and migratory aspects of professional and managerial jobs today tend to discourage the widespread utilization of women in these occupations. This is much less the case in most of the occupations in which women predominate, since the jobs tend to be fairly standardized throughout the country. As long as there are any job opportunities in urban areas, there will be some in teaching, nursing, social work, clerical work, retail sales, domestic employment, and so forth.

Summary. In general, if we review the predominantly female occupations, we find that on the whole they exhibit those characteristics promoting the attachment of the female sex label, while they tend to lack those characteristics that would favor the employment of male workers.

Consider the major female professions--nursing, teaching, librarianship, and social work. All of these depend on skilled but cheap labor in fairly large quantities, they are traditionally female occupations, most of the training for them is acquired before employment, and career continuity is not essential. They exist all over the country, and hence mobility--or the lack of it--is not usually a serious handicap. Diligence and a certain devotion to the job are required, but long-range commitments and extensive sacrifices of time and energy are not necessary. Employment in most of these occupations relatively infrequently puts the female worker in a supervisory position over male employees, though she may be in a position of relative power over those outside the organization. Nurses, for example, may initiate action for patients, but their authority to do so is derived from the attending physician;[78] furthermore, the authority and the task have a distinctly feminine flavor--that of the nurturing female. Social workers are often in power positions vis-à-vis clients, but these clients are not in the work organization and are in a notoriously poor position to effect changes anyway.

All in all, predominantly female professions tend to be lacking in characteristics discouraging the employment of women,

---

[78] Josephine Williams found, however, that female doctors were not so readily accepted ("Patients and Prejudice...," passim).

114

but well endowed with characteristics encouraging their employment. Just the opposite is the case for predominantly male pro-
fessions--law, medicine, dentistry, engineering, architecture,
university teaching and administration, and the clergy, among
others. These occupations are traditionally male--some more than
others (such as engineering, for example), but all to a considerable extent. Great investments of time, energy, and devotion
are involved in their pursuit, and extensive and often very difficult schooling, as well as a lifetime of overtime work, are
frequently associated with them. Continuity is usually essential,
and the freedom to move or to stay put, depending on the exigencies of the career, may be an important factor in whether or not
success is achieved.

With the exception of extensive schooling (though increasingly a B.A. degree is a minimum requirement, and some graduate work in business administration meets with considerable favor), the same factors of importance in male professional occupations are also important in managerial occupations--particularly
the salaried managerial. Here problems arising from utilizing
women in supervisory positions are likely to be more frequently
experienced.

Clerical work--largely female--requires cheap, but fairly
well-educated, labor. The necessary training is achieved mainly
before entrance into the labor market. It is traditionally female work, and requires characteristics supposedly more typical
of women than of men--manual dexterity, plus a tolerance of monotonous and routine tasks. Here, as in other women's jobs, a
strongly developed sense of commitment is unnecessary, geographical mobility is not essential, since clerical work is so ubiqui-
tous, and career continuity is not an important factor, because
most of the jobs have no future anyway.

Retail sales capitalizes on the cheap, available aspects
of female labor. Skill is much less a factor. Many retail jobs
are traditionally female--usually those where the customer is
expected to be a woman. None of the characteristics of predomi-
nántly male occupations seem to be in evidence here--the importance of career continuity, geographical mobility, or high motivation hardly enter into the picture. Male sales jobs, on the
other hand, differ in several important respects from female
sales jobs. If they are in retail sales, they usually involve
men's wear, or expensive items like furniture, appliances, or
jewelry. If in wholesale trade, considerable sums may be involved in each sale, because sales tend to be in quantity. Furthermore, all the male sales occupations are traditionally male
occupations. Career continuity may not be significant; however,
if the ultimate goal is to rise into a managerial position in the
company, continuity may be essential. Finally, many salesmen
have to travel quite frequently, probably one of the major factors

militating against the use of women. Women--especially married women--are usually not willing or able to leave their families frequently or for extended periods of time.

Most craft occupations in the United States are tradition-ally male, and require fairly long apprenticeships, though there is a certain amount of "stealing the trade"--acquiring training informally. Operatives jobs are more divided between the sexes--but not the same jobs. There is a very strong tendency to label certain operatives jobs female and others male, with women con-centrating in the lower paid operatives jobs. Here the presumed male (strength) or female (manual dexterity) characteristics may be important factors in sex labelling jobs. In addition, the problem of trying to have mixed work groups, or women in super-visory positions over men, may be particularly acute with semi-skilled workers.

All in all, as we have seen, there are many excellent reasons why we can expect to find the segregation of male and fe-male labor markets. What is, perhaps, surprising is not that men and women compete in separate labor markets, but rather that male labor is ever substituted for female, or female for male. Given all the factors operating to keep jobs exclusively male or ex-clusively female, why do sex labels sometimes get changed? Let us consider briefly some of the factors promoting shifts in sex labels.

Factors Promoting Changes in Job Sex Labels

There are several factors which promote the substitution of male for female, or female for male, labor. Two seem to be of outstanding importance--shifts in the nature of the job in ques-tion and labor shortages.

Changes in Nature of Job. There are at least two main reasons why the nature of a job may change: (1) there have been technological innovations which radically change its character--from hand work to operating a machine, for example--and (2) there has been a major reorganization of the work, which changes the character of the job--for example, dividing the production of an item into several components, so that workers make pieces of a product rather than the whole item. Technological innovation and work reorganization are fairly common occurrences in the indus-trialization process, and many cases can be cited of how such changes resulted in shifts in the utilization of male or female labor.

The early histories of the shoe and cotton industries provide two good examples of these processes. The shoe industry example is essentially one of changes in an industry's sex

116

composition due to a reorganization of the way a job is done, rather than to the introduction of machinery. Historically, the manufacture of boots and shoes was a male craft. In the colonial period they were made by hand, and by one man. In the latter part of the eighteenth century and the first half of the nineteenth, however, a division of labor was worked out, though all operations were still done by hand. It was soon discovered that women and children could be utilized to stitch and bind shoe uppers--little strength or skill was required for this part of the process--and so "stitching and binding" came to be exclusively women's work in the first half of the nineteenth century. After that time, the work became mechanized, but women continued to stitch and bind uppers--by machine instead of by hand, however, and in the factory instead of at home.[79]

The cotton example is one where the change is due, partially at least, to mechanization. It is also an example of the displacement of female workers by male. Between 1831 and 1905 the proportion of all cotton workers who were women declined from about 68 percent to 47 percent.[80] One of the reasons for this decline was that the introduction of heavier and faster equipment made it difficult for women to operate the machines, and facilitated the substitution of men. In addition, machine improvements increased the number of machines that could be tended by each worker.[81] Because it was easier for men than for women to take

---

[79]Abbott, Ch. VIII, "The Manufacture of Boots and Shoes," pp. 148-184.

[80]Ibid., p. 102. This decline is substantiated by Lebergott's more recent figures. He shows a decline from 63 percent female in 1830 to 39 percent female in 1909 (p. 70).

[81]Abbott traces the history of the loom: "When the power loom was first introduced, a weaver attended only a single loom and that loom ran from 80 to a 100 picks a minute. It was not long before the invention of the rotary temple made it possible for an operative to tend two looms instead of one and those looms ran at a higher speed so that the result was about 260 picks a minute. In 1850 four looms with a total of about 600 picks a minute could be watched by a single weaver. In 1895 one operative could tend eight looms which ran a total of about 1,500 picks a minute. The invention of the automatic loom enormously increased the number of looms to an operative until today a single weaver may tend as many as twenty looms running more than 4,500 picks per minute" (p. 96; the reader is reminded that this was written in 1910).

the increased load, this too was a factor in the switch from female to male labor.[82]

The introduction of the typewriter seems to have given
women their major opportunity in clerical occupations. In some
cases, of course, women or men get new job opportunities not just
because an old job has been transformed by reorganization or
mechanization, but because the rise of a new industry has created
a new job--this certainly seems to have been the case in electronics, where women are widely used for assembly work.

In sum, changes in the character of a job seem to function
mainly in two ways. First of all, they may change the requirements of the job so as to favor a switch in sexes employed. This
was obviously the case in the examples cited above. Second, if
the revision of the job is extensive, the changes constitute a
type of break with the job's tradition, and this facilitates
other breaks with tradition--such as the sex of the employee.

Labor Shortages. Little may have changed about a job,
but shortages of the traditionally preferred type of worker often
lead to the substitution of other types of workers. This certainly seems to have been the case for schoolteaching in the nineteenth century. Women were utilized when cheap native male labor
was in short supply. Again, in more recent years, shortages of
female teachers have certainly been a factor in the greater utilization of males in elementary teaching.

Probably one of the best examples of the substitution of
women for men due to labor shortages occurred during World War
II.[83] Between 1940 and 1944, female employment in general rose
about 51 percent, and the employment of women as craftsmen, foremen, operatives, and nonfarm laborers (mostly in manufacturing)

----

[82]Ibid., pp. 103ff. Abbott quotes the census in support of
this point as follows: "'The number of places in which women
can profitably be employed in a cotton mill in preference to
men, or on an equality with them, steadily decreases as the
speed of the machinery increases and as the requirement that
one hand shall tend a greater number of machines is extended'"
(p. 108).

[83]See Womanpower, Chapter 5; International Labour Organization,
The War and Women's Employment: The Experience of the United
Kingdom and the United States, Studies and Reports, New Series,
No. 1 (Montreal, 1946); and C.D. Long, Labor Force in War and
Transition, National Bureau of Economic Research Occasional Paper
No. 36 (New York, 1952).

increased by 119 percent.[84] The National Manpower Council reports:

> A 1942 study by the Women's Bureau--of 125 war plants
> engaged in the manufacture of electrical instruments,
> aircraft engines, machine and metal parts, and am-
> munition--found women concentrated in the following
> operations: assembling, machine operating, testing
> and inspecting, and packing and wrapping. Women also
> did well at riveting, welding, and blueprint reading.
> During the war, women replaced men on drill presses,
> milling machines, lathes, punch and forming presses,
> and other machine tools. During the fall of 1942 and
> the following winter, women represented from one third
> to one half of the trainees entering pre-employment
> machine shop courses. During the latter half of 1943,
> women accounted for about the same proportions of em-
> ployees entering more advanced classes in machine shop
> work.[85]

However, this substitution of women for men in traditionally male
jobs during World War II does not seem to have been permanent.
The proportion of the female labor force in operative and laboring occupations, for example, has been declining, not increasing.[86]

In general, the important point is that just as changes
in the nature of a job may challenge the traditional sex label
attached to that job, so do shortages of workers of the specified
sex. It is usually when some hitch in the traditional procedure
is experienced that innovation in the utilization of male and
female labor is most likely to occur.

Conclusion

It is time to summarize this discussion in terms of its
relevance to supply and demand. I particularly wish to focus
here on the question of demand.

---

[84] *Womanpower*, p. 158.

[85] *Ibid.*, pp. 159-160.

[86] The proportion of the female labor force in operatives occupations went down from 19.5 percent in 1940 to 16.2 percent in
1960; the proportion who were laborers declined from 1.1 percent
in 1940 to 0.6 percent in 1960 (Kaplan and Casey, Tables 6 and
6b; 1960 Census, Characteristics, Table 201).

The ready availability of cheap female labor is, of course, a supply factor. But if employers adapt themselves to such a labor supply so that the job in question acquires a "female only" label, then the demand is not just for cheap labor but for cheap _female_ labor. The job has acquired a traditional sex label, and employers will tend to follow this tradition unless some special problems arise. If, in addition, skills are required, then the employer is probably even more firmly committed to the utilization of the labor of one sex. It is hard, for example, for an employer to find a qualified male secretary, even if he should desire one. In addition, several other factors tend to make labor demands sex-specific. If presumed sex-linked characteristics are desired, such as physical strength or manual dexterity, then demand is, of course, sex-specific. If the effects of a sexually mixed work group or of having female supervisors are feared, then employer demand will tend to be sex-specific. If the desire is for a dependable, highly motivated employee who will move anywhere, then employers will tend to prefer males over females.

All those factors promoting the sex labeling of jobs tend to structure the demand for labor, though they also affect the supply. In some cases, the demand for one sex is determined by factors independent of supply. In others, the supply of one type of labor at one point in the history of the occupation affects the whole future course of the sex composition of that occupation. Whatever the particular mechanisms of a given situation, however, the existence of sex labeling of jobs means that not only does the labor supply vis-à-vis certain jobs tend to be sex-specific, but so also does the demand for labor.

Chapter 4

DIFFERENT FEMALE LABOR MARKETS

In Chapter 3 we saw that men and women tend to compete in relatively different labor markets, which implies that it is meaningful to talk about a demand for female labor as distinct from that for males. Before going on to the problem of trying to estimate the demand for female labor, and investigating how shifts in this demand may have affected the extent and pattern of female labor force participation, I would first like to differentiate the demand for female labor to some extent. For in addition to the fact that men and women do not usually operate in the same labor market, all men do not operate in one homogeneous male labor market, nor all women in a single homogeneous female market. For each sex there are a host of factors which tend to set up imperfectly competing labor markets. In this chapter, we will be concerned with two major sets of factors which differentiate female labor markets, and thus set up demands for different types of female labor. To begin with, we shall consider education, skill, and social status as important factors distinguishing female labor markets. From the demand side, employers desiring female workers have different preferences with regard to the specific skills required, educational attainment, and other social status characteristics of workers. On the supply side, women who vary in these characteristics are not equally drawn to the same types of jobs. Middle-class women, for example, are not particularly interested in manual labor. The second set of factors we shall consider concern age and marital status, for the labor market is not really the same for women of different ages and at different points in the family life cycle. In some jobs, young women are preferred to older women, for example, and in other jobs single women are preferred to married.

The question of how female labor markets are distinguished by age and marital status is particularly important because the greatest increases, as we have seen, in female labor force participation since 1940 have been for older women and for married women. This implies that the roles of age and marital status as differentiating factors in female labor markets have been changing in recent years. One aim of this chapter will be to examine these changes from the point of view of demand.

Skill, Education, and Social Status

The simple fact that the female labor force is divided up among a large number of occupations indicates that all women do not operate within the same female labor market. As we have already noted in Chapter 3, many female occupations entail certain specific skills that make it difficult to hire just any one who comes along for the job. If only for reasons of skill requirements, then, school teachers are not readily interchangeable with sewing machine operators, nurses, domestic servants, psychiatric social workers, office machine operators, and workers in many other occupations as well. However, the many occupations listed by the census exaggerate the number of labor markets thereby delimited, as there is considerable mobility among occupations. A Bureau of Labor Statistics study, for example, shows that as many as 44 percent of all job shifts by women in 1961 involved a change in occupation (Table 4.1). It is interesting to note that

Table 4.1

JOB SHIFTS OF FEMALES INVOLVING A CHANGE IN OCCUPATION:
1961

Major occupation group of job left[a]	Percent of job shifts involving a change in occupation
All job shifts by women[b]	44.1
Professional, technical and kindred workers	24.8
Clerical and kindred workers	29.5
Sales workers	67.1
Operatives and kindred workers	41.1
Service workers, except private household workers	47.8
Farm laborers and foremen	44.6
Private household workers	89.3

[a]Certain occupational categories are omitted because the bases were too small to percentage. The omitted groups are: farmers and farm managers; managers, officials, and proprietors; craftsmen, foremen and kindred workers; and laborers, except farm and mine.

[b]A job shift is defined as a change from one employer to another. A change in occupation while working for the same employer is not considered a job shift.

Source: U.S. Bureau of Labor Statistics, Special Labor Force Report, No. 35, Job Mobility in 1961, Table 10.

the proportion of shifts involving occupational changes varied
markedly from one occupational group to another. In general,
job shifts which also involved occupation shifts occurred most
frequently in the relatively unskilled occupations. At one extreme, 89 percent of the job shifts for private household workers involved a change in occupation, while at the other extreme,
only 25 percent of the shifts for professional workers took them
out of the occupational group. The great majority of manual
workers stayed in manual jobs of one sort or another, while the
great majority of nonmanual workers stayed in nonmanual jobs
(Table 4.2). For example, 90 percent of the shifts for professional and managerial workers either did not involve any change
in occupation or, if a change in occupation occurred, it was to
another nonmanual occupation.[1] In general, then, although there
may be a considerable amount of interoccupational mobility within
major groups or between groups within either the manual or the
nonmanual category, there is relatively little mobility between
the manual and nonmanual groups. These two broad occupational
groups seem to form relatively noncompeting labor markets.

There is other evidence that women operate in several
labor markets which roughly coincide with major occupational
groupings--labor markets where skill and education are major
factors. If we examine the occupational distribution of female
workers of different educational attainments, for example, it is
clear that all these women are not operating in the same labor
market (Tables 4.3 and 4.4). Most of the female labor force with
an eighth grade education or less was concentrated in manual occupations in 1960, while the majority of women with four years
of high school or more were in nonmanual jobs. Women with one
to three years of high school appear to have been in a borderline
situation, with a slight majority concentrated in manual work.
It is clear, however, that although there was some overlap, women
with very different educational attainments were generally not
operating in the same labor markets.

Expressed in terms of supply and demand, there are several obvious explanations for the differentiation of female labor
markets along the occupation-skill-education axis. Workers with
different specific skills are desired or required in many jobs
in a highly industrialized society, and as we have seen in Chapter
3, employers are hesitant to expend much time and money in on-the-
job training for women. The employer, therefore, will not make

---

[1]For earlier studies of interoccupational mobility, see Gladys L.
Palmer, Labor Mobility in Six Cities (New York: Social Science
Research Council, 1954), Chapters 1, 4, and 5; and Herbert S.
Parnes, Research on Labor Mobility (New York: Social Science Re-
search Council, 1954), Chapters 3 and 4.

Table 4.2

JOB SHIFTS OF FEMALES BY OCCUPATION GROUP OF JOB LEFT:
1961[a]

| Occupation group of job left[b] | New job | | | |
| | No change in occupation | Percent of shifts where: | | |
		Remained within manual or nonmanual category[c]	Changed to new nonmanual occupation	Changed to new manual occupation
Professional and managerial	65	90	24	10
Clerical	71	86	15	14
Sales	33	77	44	23
Operatives	59	82	18	24
Private household workers	6	79	21	73
Other service workers	53	77	23	24
Farmers and farm laborers	55	91	9	36

[a]This table refers to the number of job shifts occurring in 1961, not the number of women who changed jobs--it is possible for one woman to make several job shifts. A job shift is defined as a change from one employer to another.

[b]Craftsmen, foremen and kindred workers are not shown because the bases were too small to percentage.

[c]Professional, managerial, clerical, and sales workers were grouped together as nonmanual workers and operatives; private household workers, service workers, and farm and nonfarm laborers were grouped together as manual workers.

Source: U.S. Bureau of Labor Statistics, Special Labor Force Report, No. 35, Job Mobility in 1961, Table F.

Table 4.3

OCCUPATIONAL DISTRIBUTION OF THE EXPERIENCED CIVILIAN FEMALE LABOR FORCE, BY EDUCATIONAL ATTAINMENT: 1960

(Percent distribution)

Occupation	Total	Elementary school			High school		College		
		Under 5 years	5-7 years	8 years	1-3 years	4 years	1-3 years	4 years	5 or more years
Total, 14 years old and over	100.0	100.0	100.0	100.0	100.0	100.0	100.0	100.0	100.0
Professionals	12.5	0.6	0.9	1.6	3.2	6.8	29.6	70.3	83.6
Managers, officials, and proprietors	3.6	1.8	2.2	3.2	3.2	4.0	5.2	3.8	3.0
Farmers	0.5	1.5	1.1	1.0	0.4	0.3	0.4	0.2	0.1
Clerical workers	29.1	2.2	4.2	10.8	23.1	49.6	41.1	15.6	6.2
Sales workers	7.8	2.4	5.0	8.7	11.3	8.4	6.3	2.5	1.0
Craftsmen and foremen	1.2	0.9	1.4	1.7	1.5	1.1	0.8	0.4	0.3
Operatives	16.2	25.6	31.5	29.2	21.6	10.6	3.1	0.8	0.4
Private household workers	7.9	29.9	21.2	13.0	8.9	3.0	1.8	0.6	0.3
Other service workers	13.5	16.4	20.1	21.0	19.0	10.4	6.4	1.6	0.8
Farm laborers	1.2	5.9	3.1	2.0	1.0	0.6	0.4	0.1	0.0
Other laborers	0.6	1.4	1.1	0.8	0.7	0.4	0.2	0.0	0.0
Occupation not reported	5.8	11.2	8.1	7.0	6.1	4.8	4.7	4.0	4.3

Source: U.S. Bureau of the Census, 1960 Census of Population: Vol. I, Characteristics of the Population, Part 1, U.S. Summary, Table 201; 1960 Census of Population: Subject Report PC(2)-7A, Occupational Characteristics, Table 9.

Table 4.4

MANUAL AND NONMANUAL OCCUPATIONAL DISTRIBUTION OF THE EXPERIENCED
CIVILIAN FEMALE LABOR FORCE, BY EDUCATIONAL ATTAINMENT:
1960

(Percent distribution)

Occupation	Total	Elementary school			High school		College		
		Under 5 years	5-7 years	8 years	1-3 years	4 years	1-3 years	4 years	5 or more years
Total	100.0	100.0	100.0	100.0	100.0	100.0	100.0	100.0	100.0
Nonmanual[a]	53.0	7.0	12.3	24.3	40.8	68.8	82.2	92.2	93.8
Manual[b]	41.1	81.6	79.5	68.7	53.1	26.4	13.1	3.7	1.9
Occupation not reported	5.8	11.2	8.1	7.0	6.1	4.8	4.7	4.0	4.3

[a]Professional, managerial, clerical, and sales workers.

[b]Craftsmen and foremen, operatives, private household and other
service workers, farmers and farm laborers, and nonfarm laborers.

Source: Table 4.3.

up for too many inadequacies in pre-job training. In addition
to specific skills, employers also desire different levels of
general education for workers in different jobs. Noland and
Bakke found, for example, that 90 percent of New Haven employers
and 99 percent of Charlotte employers preferred clerical workers
to have had at least four years of high school. On the other
hand, only 30 percent of the New Haven and 51 percent of the
Charlotte employers had this preference for production workers.[2]
In general, then, women with low levels of educational attainment
and few specific skills have difficulty getting nonmanual jobs,
with the possible exception of some sales work, and hence are
concentrated in manual work. Women with at least a high school
diploma are not limited to manual jobs, of course. Since most
of these women consider themselves middle class, they probably
would not consider manual jobs even if they wanted to work and

[2]Noland and Bakke, pp. 194-195.

the family needed the money. For most middle-class women and their families, the only job opportunities that are recognized as such are in white-collar work.[3]

Age and Marital Status

In addition to a differentiation of female labor markets on the basis of education, skills, and social status, such labor markets are also differentiated by age and marital status. This is especially noticeable with regard to the demand aspect of labor markets. Marital status and age have not traditionally been a matter of indifference to all employers. This is partly because employers have, at times, shared the general view that married women take jobs away from men and single women. Adherence to this view has inspired many efforts--especially in depression times--to discriminate against married women in employment. But this has not been the only reason why married and older women have met with difficulty in finding jobs. Another is that many employers--particularly in white-collar employment--have actually preferred single and younger women on the basis of several characteristics they are thought to possess.

Public Policy and Practice. As we saw in Chapter 2, an important reason why the general public frequently expressed negative attitudes in the 1930's and 1940's toward married women working was the fear that married women took jobs away from men and single women, who, it was thought, were more in need of work. This fear seems to have been so strong that (as the reader may recall) a majority of two national samples in 1939 said they would approve bills restricting the employment of married women with husbands earning above a certain amount.[4] The Massachusetts and Illinois bills cited in the AIPO polls were by no means isolated examples of efforts to restrict the employment of married women. Shallcross reports that in the 1930's bills against married women workers were introduced in legislatures of 26 states. It is true that only one of these passed--in Louisiana, and it was later repealed[5]--but it is nevertheless significant that efforts were made in so many states and apparently (considering the two AIPO polls) with considerable popular support. Undoubtedly a major reason why these bills failed to become laws was not

---

[3]Summer jobs of students may form an exception to this, of course--for example, working as a waitress in a resort hotel.

[4]See Table 2.9.

[5]Ruth Shallcross, Should Married Women Work?, Public Affairs Pamphlet No. 49, 1940, pp. 5-6.

a lack of public backing, or even a lack of public pressure for their passage, but rather the fear that they would be declared unconstitutional by the courts. For example, Shallcross reports that in 1939 the Wisconsin Attorney General "declared unconstitutional a resolution passed by the Burnett County Board barring married women from employment."[6] The Massachusetts bill probably failed to pass for this reason too. The International Labour Review reports that in June 1939, the Massachusetts Superior Court

> advised the state legislature that the prohibition of the employment of married women in the public service while such employment was open to men and to unmarried women would violate the Massachusetts Constitution, and that the removal from public employment of all unmarried women upon marriage would violate both the Massachusetts and the Federal Constitutions. It further advised that a Bill providing that husband and wife should not at the same time be employed in the Service of the Commonwealth would discriminate against a particular class of person, in violation of the constitutional provision that all citizens had the right to equal opportunity for employment in the public service.[7]

Another example of public expression of fear of competition from married women is to be found in the history of Massachusetts. Peters reports that during the winter of 1930, the Governor of Massachusetts appointed a commission on unemployment relief. One of the major recommendations of that commission was that industrial and governmental organizations displace all married women employees living with husbands able and willing to support them, and replace them with unemployed men and single women. The Governor, in turn, urged that industrial and government organizations act in accordance with this recommendation. At least one company did so. The New England Telephone Company, a subsidiary of the American Telephone and Telegraph Company, started to follow the recommendation. They did not go far in carrying out the plan, however, for as Peters puts it, "the disruption in their organizations was too costly to justify it as a relief measure."[8] The

---

[6] Ibid., p. 27.

[7] "Discrimination in Employment or Occupation on the Basis of Marital Status," II, International Labour Review, LXXXV (April 1962), p. 378.

[8] David W. Peters, The Status of the Married Woman Teacher (New York: Bureau of Publications, Teachers College, Columbia University, 1934), p. 9.

fact that a responsible public body made such a recommendation and that, furthermore, some effort was made to carry it out is indicative of how well accepted the view was that the employment of married women constituted an economic threat to other workers.

Perhaps the best documented case of discrimination against married women as a matter of public policy is in the teaching profession. The National Education Association has data on the hiring and firing policies of public school districts throughout the country from the late 1920's to the 1950's. Table 4.5 summarizes

Table 4.5

POLICIES REGARDING THE EMPLOYMENT OF MARRIED WOMEN AS TEACHERS: 1928-1956

(percent distribution of replies for all reporting cities with a population of 2,500 or more)

	1928	1930	1941	1950	1956
Employing married women as new teachers:					
Yes	39	23	13	82	97
No	61	77	58	8	--
Rarely, under special conditions, including responsibility for dependents	--[a]	--[a]	29	10	4
Single women teachers who marry:					
Required to resign	51	61	61	--[a]	--[a]
At once	25	33	28	--[a]	--
At end of school year	26	28	33	--[a]	--
May continue to teach	48	37	30	--[a]	97[a]
Other[b]	2	2	9	--[a]	--[a]

[a]Not available.

[b]Includes not reported and practice varies.

Sources: National Education Association Bulletin: "Practices Affecting Teacher Personnel," 6 (Sept. 1928), p. 221; "Administrative Practices Affecting Classroom Teachers, Part I: The Selection and Appointment of Teachers," 10 (Jan. 1932), p. 19; "Teacher Personnel Procedures: Selection and Appointment," 20 (March 1942), p. 60, and 20 (May 1942), p. 107; "Teacher Personnel Practices, 1950-51: Appointment and Termination of Service," 30 (Feb. 1952), p. 12; International Labour Review, "Discrimination in Employment or Occupation on the Basis of Marital Status," II, LXXXV (April 1962), p. 372, and I, LXXXV (March 1962), p. 268.

the situation. Even before the 1929 crash, the majority of school
systems would not hire married women as teachers, and about half
required single teachers to resign upon marriage--25 percent immediately and 26 percent at the end of the school year. By 1930
the situation had tightened still further. Only 23 percent of
the school systems reporting would hire married women as teachers,
and 61 percent required single women teachers to resign upon mar-
riage--33 percent at once and 28 percent at the end of the school
year. The discrimination against married women was even more
pronounced in 1941. Then, only 13 percent of the school systems
would hire married women--58 percent said they would not hire
them at all, and 29 percent said they would hire married women
only rarely, under special conditions, such as responsibility of
the woman for dependents. About the same proportion of school
systems in 1941 as in 1930--61 percent--required single teachers
to resign upon marriage. However, there was an increase in variable policies and a decrease in the proportion of school systems
which had a general policy of allowing the single woman to stay
on after marriage--from 37 percent in 1930 to 30 percent in 1941.

One of the major reasons given for this discrimination
against married women teachers was, of course, that teaching jobs
should go to those who must support themselves.[9] It was also
argued, however, that compared to single women, married women
were generally less efficient and less satisfactory as teachers.
This was because they were, it was thought, more preoccupied with
home interests. Second, it was argued that, being less dependent
on their jobs, they felt more independent of the educational authorities, and were not willing to assume their share of responsibility in the school. Third, it was argued that married women
tend to stagnate professionally--they are, for example, unwilling
or do not have the time to obtain additional professional training.
Finally, it was said that it was difficult to remove married women,
even if they were obviously inefficient, because, due to their
local residence, they had influence through friends and relations
who could hamper school authorities.[10] There was, thus, a certain

---

[9] For a discussion of the reasons behind these discriminatory
policies, see National Education Association, "Administrative
Practices Affecting Classroom Teachers, Part I: The Selection
and Appointment of Teachers," Research Bulletin, X (Jan. 1932),
pp. 1-33; "Teacher Personnel Procedures: Selection and Appointment," ibid., XX (March 1942), pp. 51-79.

[10] National Education Association, 1932 study. There were, in addition, reasons given that had to do not with the teacher work role
but with the homemaker role. For example, it was argued that married women teachers would neglect their home and families, and
that permitting married women to work tended to reduce the birth
rate. See both the 1932 and 1942 NEA studies.

amount of prejudice against married women because it was felt that they did not make as good or as tractable teachers as single women.

In the 1920's, 1930's, and 1940's, there were, therefore, very widespread policies against hiring married women as teachers, and policies requiring the resignation of single teachers who marry. By 1950, however, these policies were rapidly ending (Table 4.5). In 1950, for example, the National Education Association found that 82 percent of school districts (as compared to 13 percent in 1941) hired married women as new teachers. By 1956, 97 percent of school districts did so. Furthermore, while only 30 percent of single teachers who married were permitted to continue to teach in 1941, by 1956, 97 percent were allowed to do so. Bars against hiring or keeping married women in the teaching profession had thus been virtually wiped out by 1956.

The reasons for this dramatic change are not difficult to see. Protests against the injustice of discriminating against married women in the teaching profession may have had some effect, but there seems little doubt that the major factor in eliminating such practices has been the acute teacher shortages starting with the entrance of the baby-boom children into the school system.[11] Discriminatory policies against married women are a luxury few school systems in the United States can afford today. No longer is there an abundance of teachers and a shortage of pupils. Today, restrictions on the employment of married women teachers would help no one; they would only make the problem of staffing the nation's schools even more difficult than it already is.

Private Policy and Practice. There is some evidence that an important factor guiding hiring policies in private, as well as public, employment during the 1930's was the view that only married women in need should be hired. The National Federation of Business and Professional Women's Clubs made a survey early in 1940 of local employment policies. This survey (based largely on small communities) showed that married women were most likely to find bars against them if they sought jobs as school teachers, or as office workers in public utilities or large manufacturing concerns.[12] To be more specific, the Federation found that 43 percent of the public utilities, 29 percent of the large manufacturing concerns, 23 percent of the small private businesses, and 13 percent of the department stores had bars against married

---

[11]See National Education Association, "Teacher Personnel Practices, 1950-51: Appointment and Termination of Service," Research Bulletin, XXX (Feb. 1952), pp. 12-13.

[12]Shallcross, pp. 6-7.

women.[13] Although relatively few department stores discriminated
in 1939, the Department Store Economist reported that the senti-
ment against married women "is growing stronger." Opposition,
it was found, came from customers, labor organizations, women's
clubs, and miscellaneous groups of the unemployed.[14]

There is also a relevant study published in 1939 by the
National Industrial Conference Board (NICB). The general conclusion was that

> private employers, on the whole, have considered merit
> more important than marital status. However, the
> study reveals some tendency on the part of employers
> to be influenced by the current belief that the un-
> employment problem can be solved if married women are
> hired only in need. Approximately 60 percent of the
> companies studied by the Board report no restrictions
> against married women who work in offices. But there
> are some fields where they do face serious handicaps.
> For example, 84 percent of the insurance companies,
> 65 percent of the public utilities, as compared with
> 14 percent of manufacturing concerns and 11 percent
> of mercantile establishments, had restrictions against
> the employment of married women in offices.[15]

In general, then, although hiring policies which discriminated against married women in private employment were by no
means universal in the 1930's, they were nevertheless quite common
in certain industries and occupations. Fear that working married
women deprived needy persons of jobs was not the only factor operating in the situation. There were other reasons why there were
hiring policies which were unfavorable to married women.

There is also evidence that discrimination against older
women has been fairly common. Noland and Bakke's extensive study
of hiring policies in New Haven and Charlotte in 1945 and 1946
provides some information on preferences for young, single women.[1]

---

[13]Ibid., p. 9.

[14]Ibid., pp. 6-7.

[15]Ibid., p. 9.

[16]Noland and Bakke's study was limited to industrial firms, and
hence excludes firms in the service fields. Judging from the
earlier NICB and National Federation of Business and Professional
Women's Clubs studies, this would seem to indicate that the Noland
and Bakke study might underestimate the prevalence of discriminato

The study gives employer requirements and preferences by several types of jobs--e.g., production work, routine clerical work, administrative and executive work--and it is not always possible to separate preferred or required characteristics for female, as opposed to male, workers. However, as we have already seen, most employers preferred women for routine clerical work,[17] so that employer preferences for this occupational category probably accurately reflect preferences for certain types of female workers.[18]

Noland and Bakke reported that 35 percent of the New Haven employers and as many as 47 percent of the Charlotte employers had preferences regarding the family status of clerical workers. Of those that had preferences, 80 percent of the New Haven employers and 60 percent of the Charlotte employers preferred to have their clerical workers single.[19] Thus, a fairly substantial minority of employers in both cities preferred single clerical workers.

The attitudes towards preferred age of workers were much more definite, however. Fully 77 percent of the New Haven and 91 percent of the Charlotte employers had opinions on the best age of all workers at time of hiring. Seventy-eight percent of the New Haven and 92 percent of the Charlotte employers with opinions on the subject thought the best age was under 35. This was the average for all kinds of jobs combined, and it was a general preference, regardless of the sex of the worker. For routine clerical work, 74 percent of the New Haven and 88 percent of the Charlotte employers expressed opinions on the subject--of

---

hiring policies, since these other studies found considerable discrimination in some of the service fields. Given these limitations, however, the Noland and Bakke study seems quite a thorough one of its chosen universe--135 establishments in New Haven and 105 in Charlotte. All plants employing more than 500 persons and one in five of the remainder were included in the survey. The establishments covered employed about 80 percent of the industrial labor force in the two metropolitan areas (see their Appendix A, pp. 173-174).

[17]See p. 104 in Chapter 3.

[18]That this is the case is indicated by the fact that when employers give the reasons for their preferences for certain types of clerical workers, these reasons are almost always couched in terms of characteristics of female workers.

[19]This includes all those who prefer all their clerical workers single, and those who prefer the clerical workers single if they are females (Noland and Bakke, p. 204).

these, 95 percent of the New Haven and 99 percent of the Charlotte employers thought the best age for hiring clerical workers was under 35. In fact, 74 percent of the New Haven and 82 percent of the Charlotte employers who expressed opinions preferred to hire clerical workers under age 25.[20] There was, then, a very strong preference for young clerical workers indicated.

Several reasons were given by employers for preferring younger women, and for not wanting older women. For one thing, it was argued that very young clerical workers--those under 22 years of age, for example--were more easily trained and more inclined to accept the company's way of doing things. Second, it was thought that young workers were more mentally alert, stronger, more attractive and ornamental than older women. It was also argued that young workers could be started at lower wages, and hence rewarded by increases more frequently as a spur to their efforts. Furthermore, it was thought that hiring young girls would mean that their service would less likely be interrupted by weddings and babies--at least for a while.[21] In general, it was felt that women "begin to decline in physical stamina and become 'neurotic' after forty,"[22] and that older women were less attractive. Finally, it was argued that most clerical workers on a staff were going to be young people, and hence older workers would not fit in. It was said, for example, that

> most women leave employment when they are married and
> the rest of the staff is inclined to label them as
> "not really having made a go of marriage," if they
> continue to work beyond forty. If they have not mar-
> ried, they are still more likely to be considered as
> "different."[23]

Some negative attitudes toward hiring older women have persisted into the 1950's. In the course of its womanpower study, the National Manpower Council held seven conferences in different parts of the country to gather data from employers on, among other things, hiring policies.[24] The conferees were selected "so as to

---

[20]Ibid., p. 200.

[21]Ibid., p. 70.

[22]Ibid., p. 69.

[23]Ibid.

[24]Conferences were held in Boston, New York, St. Louis, Chicago, Los Angeles, San Francisco, and Asheville, North Carolina. See Womanpower, Ch. III, "Women in Business and Industry: An Employer Appraisal," pp. 86-109.

insure that different kinds of enterprises in which women constitute a significant proportion of the work force were represented."[25] The Council reported that many employers set a limit on
the age at which they were willing to hire women. For some, the
maximum age was 30 or 35, and a few would not hire women over
26--or even 21. Pension considerations were said to be an important reason why companies prefer to hire young workers. It was
also argued that older women were often set in their ways and
found it difficult to get along with fellow workers and superi-
ors.[26]

However, whatever the _attitudes_ may be now, or whatever
they may have been since the 1940's, it is obvious that discriminatory policies against married women and older women must have
been considerably reduced in the 1940's and 1950's. Otherwise
the enormous expansion of the married female labor force, and of
the labor force of the older women, could not have taken place.
There is some direct evidence of this in statements of hiring
policies and preferences. Ginder found, in a 1958 National Office
Management Association (NOMA) study of hiring policies in New York,
San Francisco, and Houston, that only 9 percent of the firms in
New York set a maximum age of 35 or less for women office workers.
The percentage in San Francisco was only 3.5, but 27 percent of
the Houston firms had this maximum. Discriminatory policies in-
creased fairly quickly after age 35, however--especially in
Houston. For example, 26 percent of the New York firms set maxi-
mum hiring ages between 35 and 45 years of age, as did 40 percent
of the San Francisco firms and 66 percent of the Houston firms.
Altogether, 54 percent of the New York firms, 72 percent of the
San Francisco firms, and 73 percent of the Houston firms set the
maximum at between 35 and 50.[27] In general, Ginder's study indicates maximum hiring ages much higher than in the Noland and
Bakke study of the 1940's. Nevertheless, there seemed to be an
accelerating disinclination to hire women between the ages of 35
and 50--especially in Houston and San Francisco. These results
seem particularly interesting when we remember that the peak labor force rates of women in 1960 were for those 45-49 years old,
and that labor force rates for women, by five-year age intervals
within the 35-54 range, were usually higher than for women at
most ages below 35 (Table 1.3). The policies of employers did

---

[25]_Ibid._, p. 87.

[26]_Ibid._, p. 103.

[27]Charles E. Ginder, "Chapter Surveys Give Comparative Data on
Discrimination Against Older Workers in New York, San Francisco,
Houston," _Office Executive,_ 33 (October 1958), p. 43.

not seem to be keeping ahead of the actualities, but rather lagging somewhat behind.[28]

These findings--relating to only three cities--may not be representative, of course. A national survey was conducted by NOMA in 1960, however, and covered 1,991 business, industrial, and service organizations in the United States and Canada.[29] The study indicates that only 8 percent of the companies did not hire women past 35, which was not very different from the New York figures in the 1958 NOMA survey. Twenty-eight percent of the firms in the 1960 survey only occasionally hired women past 35; 64 percent hired women over 35 for office positions.[30] The two surveys are not quite comparable, because the questions asked were different, but the 1960 survey does not indicate significantly more liberal policies than the 1958 survey, though both, of course, indicate a much wider practice of hiring older women. Unfortunately, there is no information in the 1960 survey on just how much beyond age 35 the companies were willing to go.

On the whole, then, there has been a general shift away from hiring policies which discriminate against married or older women in private, as well as in public, employment. The liberalization of hiring policies has permitted the employment of a large group of women whose previous employment prospects were relatively poor. This suggests that a shift in employer demand was an important factor in the post-1940 changes in the age pattern of female labor force participation. In teaching, clerical work, and many other occupations, married women and older women have seen their employment opportunities increased greatly in the past twenty years. The evidence is that they responded to these opportunities by entering the labor force in large numbers. What caused these changes in hiring policies? Our discussion of public school teaching suggests that such policy shifts might initially, at least, have been in response to labor shortages.

---

[28] Job discrimination against the older worker is by no means limited to women, of course. For a recent study of such discrimination towards both men and women, see U.S. Secretary of Labor, The Older American Worker: Age Discrimination in Employment, 2 vols. (Washington: U.S. Department of Labor, 1965). This study indicates that women, recently at least, have been faring somewhat better than men as far as meeting with age discrimination is concerned (Vol. II: Research Materials, pp. 5-9).

[29] Of the firms studied, 355 were in Canada. See Charles E. Ginder, "Factor of Sex in Office Employment," Office Executive, 36 (February 1961), pp. 10-13.

[30] Ibid., p. 13.

In private employment, too, the evidence seems to point to the conclusion that hiring policies have been modified as an accommodation to rather acute shortages of the more traditionally preferred type of female worker--the young single girl. Employers have often turned to hiring married women and older women not so much because they have independently discovered the worth of such women, but because they cannot get enough young single women. However, after using older women for a while, many employers have discovered that in comparison with younger women, the older ones did not have so many handicaps after all. In fact, they may even have several virtues that younger girls may not generally possess. This realization, of course, tends to break down still further the barriers against hiring older women.

That labor shortages have been an important factor influencing hiring policies is indicated by several studies. Ginder found, for example, that of the companies in the 1960 NOMA study who did not hire women past 35 for office positions, or only occasionally did so (36 percent of all companies studied), 65 percent were considering reevaluating this practice, because they thought that workers in this age group would be the principal source of supply in the near future.[31] Miriam Hussey, in a study of the Philadelphia female labor market in 1957,[32] reported that

firms accustomed to depending on high school graduates for their new recruits in occupations primarily filled by women have been hard put to it to find and retain personnel. Office workers have been especially scarce, so that banks, insurance companies, and utility firms are among those severely affected.[33]

There were varied responses to these shortages in Philadelphia, according to Hussey. One was to intensify recruitment efforts and to raise wages and increase fringe benefits.

---

[31]Ibid., p. 13.

[32]Personnel Policies During a Period of Shortage of Young Women Workers in Philadelphia (Industrial Research Unit, Wharton School of Finance and Commerce, University of Pennsylvania, 158). The data for this study came from over 50 interviews with personnel officers of large firms selected from 14 industries known to be major employers of women in clerical, selling, and production occupations. The companies represented in the study, directly or indirectly, employed about 80,000 women, or about half of all women serving as office workers, sales clerks, or factory operatives in Philadelphia.

[33]Ibid., p. 3.

These responses, of course, only increase competition; they do
not provide a collective solution to the problem of shortages.
Other steps were taken, however. One was to make an effort to
further automate operations. In addition, Hussey notes, the ban
on employing married women had generally been dropped during the
war, and those companies that "had continued the policy gave it
up when they could not maintain work forces composed solely of
single women."[34] Commenting on changes in hiring policies regarding older workers, Hussey remarks that "companies that do
not adhere strictly to a principle of promotion from within have
found that hiring older women solves some of their shortage problems."[35] Rearranging work loads so that more part-time work was
available was another solution[36]--this, of course, greatly facilitates the use of married women. In general, all sorts of methods
were used to cope with shortages, but the most important seem to
have been those which made possible or facilitated the employment
of married women and older women.

Once employers began to hire married and older women
workers--if for no other reason than that they had to--they discovered that older women had certain advantages relative to younger women. This was partly because of changes in the younger group
and partly because employers found older women different from what
they had expected. The advantages of hiring younger women have
been rapidly decreasing. For the most part, the economy has been
very prosperous since the war, and jobs have been easy for single
women to find. Hence they, as well as married women, could be
relatively independent of any one job. Instead of being more
dependable than married women, they have frequently been found
to be less so;[37] their chief interest is often finding a husband,
and they do not worry much about keeping their jobs or being
conscientious.[38]

---

[34]Ibid., p. 5.

[35]Ibid., p. 18.

[36]Ibid., p. 21.

[37]One study of Philadelphia office workers by the NOMA revealed
that turnover was higher for single than for married women (ibid.,
pp. 14-15).

[38]Hussey points out that "carelessness in [the] appearance [of
younger workers] and indifference to work responsibilities disturbed some personnel managers to the point of making them willing
to hire older women whose attitudes and work habits more than offset the disadvantages of part-time schedules and perhaps a slower
rate of production" (ibid., p. 18).

The 1960 NOMA study found that the main reasons given by the 64 percent of the companies who hired women over 35 were that older women were more stable and dependable, they were equal to or better than younger workers, and there was less turnover among them.[39]

Employing married women or older women, then, has proved to be a feasible solution to shortages of young single women. In fact, not only has it turned out to be a feasible solution, but many employers have discovered that older women offer certain advantages not always obtainable from young girls.

Conclusion

The main purpose of this chapter has been to show that several female labor markets are distinguishable. In this way, I have tried to lay the groundwork for a more refined analysis of the shifting demands for female workers, and the effects of these shifts on the female labor force. My concern has been, first of all, to show that female labor markets can be differentiated on the basis of skill and education. Such a differentiation implies that female labor markets are also differentiated according to social status, because this is closely related to educational attainment. The occupational differentiation of the female labor force, labor mobility patterns, and the uneven occupational distribution of women with different educational attainments all indicate that a multiplicity of female labor markets are in operation. The main reason on the demand side for this proliferation of female labor markets is that employers have varied desires regarding the skill, education, and social status of female workers for different jobs. On the supply side, it is that lower-class women generally do not qualify for white-collar jobs, while middle-class women do qualify. Since middle-class women have a pronounced distaste for manual labor outside the home, except under very special circumstances, they tend to concentrate in white-collar work.

Female labor markets are distinguished not only according to education and skill, but also according to age and marital status. Although the data are rather fragmentary, the evidence is that in the 1930's and 1940's discriminatory hiring policies

---

[39]Ginder, "Factor of Sex...," p. 12. Studies of employee turnover indicate that, in general, older workers--both men and women--have lower turnover rates than younger workers (see U.S. Bureau of Labor Statistics, Special Labor Force Report, No. 35, Job Mobility in 1961, p. 4; Parnes, Ch. 4, "Some Determinants of Labor Mobility," pp. 100ff.).

were fairly common against married women and women past 35, most of whom are married. This was especially true in clerical work and teaching. Such discriminatory practices have, to a considerable extent, been disappearing, and this has probably been an important factor in the increased employment of older and married women. This liberalization of hiring policies seems to have been precipitated by the shortage of young women, both single and married without young children.

Our next task is to consider what effect shifts in the occupational and industrial composition of demand in the United States has had on the female labor force. Our investigation will depend partly on the analysis of male and female labor markets in Chapter 3, and partly on the analysis of the multiplicity of female labor markets in this chapter.

Chapter 5

THE INTERACTION OF DEMOGRAPHIC AND ECONOMIC FACTORS IN
THE GROWTH OF THE FEMALE LABOR FORCE

Chapters 3 and 4 have been a necessary prelude to an
analysis of the trend in the demand for female labor, and the
possible effects of this demand on the female work rate. The
main purpose of Chapter 3 was to show that the idea of a demand
for _female_ labor has validity. In general, the argument followed
two main lines. First of all, it was shown that women concentrate
in jobs composed largely of female workers. Second, it was noted
that these jobs tend to acquire feminine sex labels, and the labels persist through time. Now if the demand for workers in
particular types of jobs necessarily entails a demand for _female_
labor, then an investigation of the long-term trends in the growth
of various occupations and industries should give us some insight
into shifts in the demand for female labor. For example, if occupations with a feminine sex label have been expanding rapidly,
we may take this expansion as a rough indicator of an expansion
in the demand for female labor. Our first task in this chapter,
then, will be to investigate trends in industrial and occupational growth, with the objective of determining the implications of
these trends for the demand for female labor and, ultimately, the
implications for the size of the female labor force. After this
matter is dealt with, we can go on to the rather perplexing problem of why age patterns of female employment have shifted radically in the postwar years.

Industrial and Occupational Shifts Since 1900

The twentieth century has seen considerable differentials
in the growth of employment in various industries in the United
States. As a result, the industrial composition of the American
labor force has undergone great changes. Although total employment has been increasing at a rapid rate, the number employed in
agriculture has been declining since 1910 (Chart 5.1); on the
other hand, employment in manufacturing and service industries
has been expanding rapidly. The rate of growth in the service
industries, in particular, has been noteworthy. The result of
these overall trends is that the proportion of workers in agriculture has declined drastically--from 42 percent in 1900 to less
than 10 percent in 1960 (Table 5.1). The proportion of workers
in manufacturing and services has been rising. The service sector has become the most important numerically of the three

CHART 5.1. EMPLOYED, BY THREE TYPES OF INDUSTRY GROUPS:
1900-1960

(in millions)

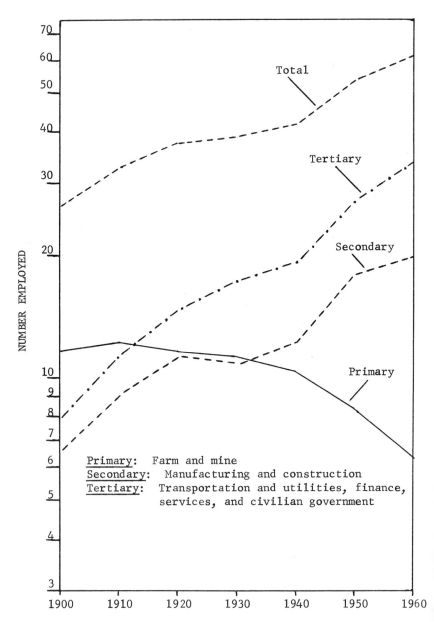

Primary: Farm and mine
Secondary: Manufacturing and construction
Tertiary: Transportation and utilities, finance,
services, and civilian government

Source: Derived from Stanley Lebergott, Manpower in Economic Growth
(New York: McGraw-Hill Book Co., 1964), pp. 514-515.

Table 5.1

INDUSTRY GROUPS OF THE EMPLOYED:
1900-1960

(Percent distribution)

Industry	1900	1910	1920	1930	1940	1950	1960
Total employed	100.0	100.0	100.0	100.0	100.0	100.0	100.0
Primary industries	44.5	37.4	30.7	28.5	25.0	15.9	10.7
Farm	42.1	34.2	27.6	26.0	22.8	14.2	9.5
Mining	2.4	3.2	3.1	2.5	2.2	1.7	1.2
Secondary industries	25.2	27.9	30.4	27.4	29.3	33.3	32.7
Construction	4.4	4.1	2.2	33.4	3.1	4.4	4.8
Manufacturing	20.8	23.8	28.2	24.0	26.2	28.9	27.9
Tertiary industries	30.2	34.7	38.9	44.0	45.7	50.6	56.6
Transportation and utilities	8.7	10.2	11.4	9.3	7.2	7.6	6.7
Trade	9.5	10.8	10.6	14.6	16.1	17.8	19.0
Finance	1.2	1.5	2.4	3.7	3.6	3.6	4.5
Services	6.6	7.3	8.2	8.5	8.8	10.2	12.2
Civilian government	4.2	4.9	6.3	7.9	10.0	11.4	14.2

Source: Derived from Stanley Lebergott, Manpower in Economic Growth (New York: McGraw-Hill Book Co., 1964), Tables A-5 and A-6.

industry groupings, and has shown the most consistent rate of increase in employment.

Unfortunately, data on the industry of the employed, by sex, is available only since 1940. These data indicate that, on the whole, the trends for men and women considered separately parallel those for employed male and female workers combined (Table 5.2, Charts 5.1 and 5.2). The interesting differences are largely those of degree. Thus, the type of industrial composition that employed males have been approaching is one that was earlier characteristic of the female labor force. The proportion of females employed in agriculture, for example, was already under 5 percent in 1940, while 24 percent of males were still in this category. Furthermore, the growing tendency of male workers to concentrate in service industries was already typical of women in 1940. Since 1940, and probably for some years before, a large majority of female workers have been concentrated in this sector, while hardly 50 percent of employed males in 1960 were in service industries. However, within this sector as a whole, there were significant changes in the industrial

THE FEMALE LABOR FORCE IN THE UNITED STATES

Table 5.2

INDUSTRY GROUPS OF THE EMPLOYED, BY SEX:
1940-1960

(Percent distribution)[a]

Industry	Males			Females		
	1940	1950	1960	1940	1950	1960
Total employed	100.0	100.0	100.0	100.0	100.0	100.0
Primary industries	26.8	18.2	10.8	4.6	4.1	2.3
Agriculture, forestry and fishing	24.0	16.0	9.3	4.5	3.9	2.1
Mining	2.7	2.2	1.4	0.1	0.2	0.2
Secondary industries	30.8	35.8	40.0	21.7	24.3	22.6
Construction	6.1	8.4	8.7	0.3	0.6	0.7
Manufacturing	24.7	27.4	31.3	21.4	23.7	21.8
Tertiary industries	42.3	45.9	49.2	73.7	71.8	75.0
Transportation, communication and other utilities	8.3	9.3	8.8	3.1	4.5	3.8
Wholesale and retail trade	16.5	17.3	17.6	18.7	23.1	21.8
Finance, insurance, and real estate	3.0	2.8	3.5	4.2	5.1	6.1
Business and repair services	2.4	2.8	3.0	0.7	1.0	1.7
Private household services	0.8	0.5	0.4	19.0	9.0	8.6
Other personal services	2.6	2.4	2.2	7.2	5.9	5.1
Entertainment and recreation	1.0	0.9	0.8	0.8	0.8	0.7
Professional and related services	4.3	5.1	7.3	17.2	18.1	22.6
Public administration	3.2	4.6	5.5	2.9	4.3	4.5

[a]Unknowns were allocated according to the distribution of knowns.

Sources: Derived from U.S. Bureau of the Census, 1960 Census of Population: Vol. I, Characteristics of the Population, Part 1, U.S Summary, Table 211; 1950 Census of Population: Vol. II, Characteristics of the Population, Part 1, U.S. Summary, Table 131.

CHART 5.2. EMPLOYED, BY THREE TYPES OF INDUSTRY GROUPS,
BY SEX: 1940-1960

(in millions)

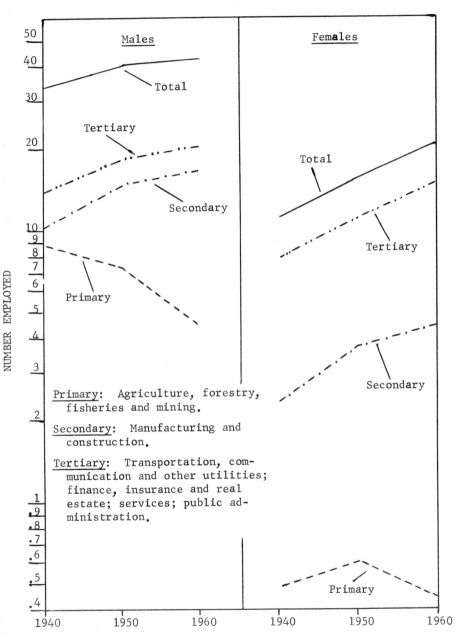

Sources: Derived from U.S. Bureau of the Census, 1950 Census of
Population: Vol. II, Characteristics of the Population, Part 1,
U.S. Summary, Table 131; 1960 Census of Population: Vol. I,
Characteristics of the Population, Part 1, U.S. Summary, Table
211.

distribution of men and women in the 1940-1960 period. Most no-
table were the changes in the private household and personal
services fields. In 1940, women were heavily concentrated in
these two industry categories, but they were of very low importance for men in the 1940-1960 period. These industries have
considerably declined in importance for women since 1940. In
this respect, then, the industrial distribution of females has
converged toward the male distribution. In general, however, in
spite of some important differences in the detailed industrial
distributions of men and women in the three major industrial
groups, the female labor force is what one might term supertypical of the general trends exhibited by male workers.

The occupational composition of the labor force is, as we
might expect, closely related to its industrial composition, since
different industries tend to have different occupational struc-
tures. In manufacturing, construction, and mining, a high proportion of the workers are operatives, craftsmen, or foremen.
On the other hand, a high proportion of the employees in public
administration and professional services are professionals or
other white-collar workers. As a result of industry differences
in occupational composition, we would therefore expect that shifts
in industrial composition would necessarily lead to shifts in occupational composition. In addition to the effects of inter-
industry shifts on occupational composition, there have been important effects from intra-industry changes as well. The trend
toward large corporations and big government tends to increase
the proportions in clerical and salaried managerial work, and
the increasingly technical nature of life in an industrial society
puts a high premium on professional and technical occupations within all industry groups. On both counts, then--because of intra-
as well as inter-industry changes--the occupational distributions
of the male and female work forces have undergone considerable
changes in the past sixty years.

First and foremost, there has been a tremendous decline
in the proportion, and even the number, of workers in the farm
occupations (Table 5.3 and Chart 5.3). Second, there has been a
general shift from manual to nonmanual occupations. Finally,
workers have become increasingly concentrated--within both the
manual and nonmanual categories--in the more skilled occupations.
This is indicated by the decline in the importance of unskilled
labor, the increasing proportions in the craftsman-foreman group
(for men only, however), and the growth of professional and technical occupations. All these changes are what we would expect
considering the growth of service industries on the one hand, and
on the other, the increasing reliance of all industry groups on
technology and the bureaucratic method of organization.

On the basis of our analysis of the segregation of male
and female labor markets in Chapter 3, we would expect that the

Table 5.3

OCCUPATIONAL DISTRIBUTION OF THE LABOR FORCE:
1900, 1940, AND 1960

Major occupation group	Percent distribution		
	1900	1940	1960[a]
Total	100.0	100.0	100.0
Farm occupations	37.4	17.4	6.0
Farmers and farm managers	19.6	10.4	3.7
Farm laborers and foremen	17.6	7.0	2.3
Nonfarm occupations	62.3	82.7	89.1
Manual occupations	44.8	51.6	48.9
Craftsmen, foremen and kindred workers	10.5	12.0	13.6
Operatives and kindred workers	12.8	18.4	18.9
Laborers	12.5	9.4	5.2
Private household workers	5.4	4.7	2.7
Other service workers	3.6	7.1	8.5
Nonmanual occupations	17.5	31.1	40.2
Professional, technical and kindred workers	4.2	7.5	10.8
Managers, officials and proprietors	5.8	7.3	8.1
Clerical and kindred workers	3.0	9.6	14.2
Sales workers	4.5	6.7	7.1

[a]Percentages do not add up to 100.0 because of 5.1 percent with occupation unknown in 1960.

Sources: Derived from D.L. Kaplan and M.C. Casey, Occupational Trends in the United States, 1900 to 1950, Bureau of the Census Working Paper No. 5, Table 6; U.S. Bureau of the Census, 1960 Census of Population: Vol. I, Characteristics of the Population, Part 1, U.S. Summary, Table 201.

male and female work forces would exhibit both different occupational distributions and different trends in occupational growth. To some extent, this is the case. Nevertheless, in spite of important differences in occupational composition and occupational growth, the major trends for both men and women are quite similar (Table 5.4 and Chart 5.4). For men as well as women, there were both a relative and an absolute decline in the numbers engaged in farm occupations. For both there was a rapid growth of employment in nonfarm occupations, and for both the rate of growth

CHART 5.3. THE FARM-NONFARM AND MANUAL-NONMANUAL LABOR FORCE: 1900-1960

(in millions)

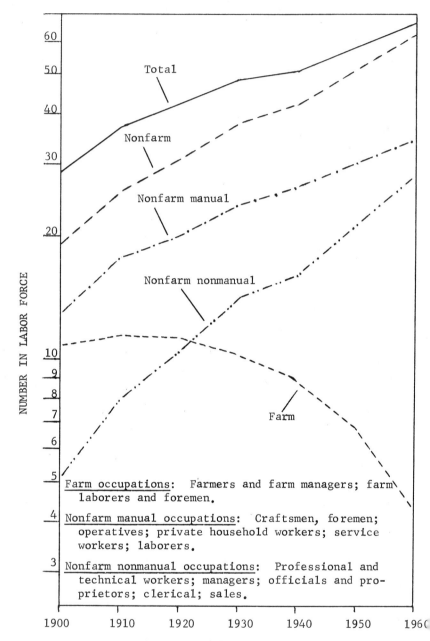

Farm occupations: Farmers and farm managers; farm laborers and foremen.

Nonfarm manual occupations: Craftsmen, foremen; operatives; private household workers; service workers; laborers.

Nonfarm nonmanual occupations: Professional and technical workers; managers; officials and proprietors; clerical; sales.

Sources: Derived from D.L. Kaplan and M.C. Casey, Occupational Trends in the United States, 1900 to 1950, Table 6; U.S. Bureau of the Census, 1960 Census of Population: Vol. I, Characteristics of the Population, Part 1, U.S. Summary, Table 201.

Table 5.4

OCCUPATIONAL DISTRIBUTION OF THE LABOR FORCE, BY SEX:
1900, 1940, AND 1960

	Percent distribution					
	Males			Females		
Major occupation group	1900	1940	1960[a]	1900	1940	1960[a]
Total	100.0	100.0	100.0	100.0	100.0	100.0
Farm occupations	41.7	21.7	8.1	19.0	4.0	1.7
Farmers and farm managers	23.0	13.3	5.3	5.9	1.2	0.5
Farm laborers and foremen	18.7	8.4	2.8	13.1	2.8	1.2
Nonfarm occupations	58.3	78.3	87.0	81.0	96.0	92.4
Manual occupations	40.7	51.7	53.3	63.1	51.1	39.4
Craftsmen, foremen and kindred workers	12.6	15.5	19.6	1.4	1.1	1.2
Operatives and kindred workers	10.3	18.1	20.2	23.7	19.5	16.2
Laborers	14.7	12.1	7.4	2.6	1.1	0.6
Private household workers	0.2	0.3	0.1	28.7	18.1	7.9
Other service workers	2.9	5.7	6.0	6.7	11.3	13.5
Nonmanual occupations	17.6	26.6	33.7	17.9	44.9	53.0
Professional, technical and kindred workers	3.4	5.8	9.9	8.2	12.8	12.5
Managers, officials and proprietors	6.8	8.6	10.3	1.4	3.3	3.6
Clerical and kindred workers	2.8	5.8	6.8	4.0	21.4	29.1
Sales workers	4.6	6.4	6.7	4.3	7.4	7.8

[a]The 1960 percentages do not add up to 100.0 because 4.7 percent of the men and 5.8 percent of the women had no occupation listed.

Sources: Gertrude Bancroft, The American Labor Force (New York: John Wiley & Sons, 1958), Table D-2; U.S. Bureau of the Census, 1960 Census of Population: Vol. I, Characteristics of the Population, Part 1, U.S. Summary, Table 201.

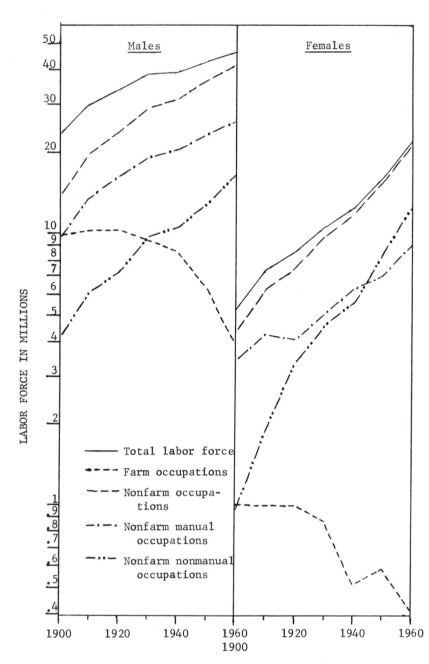

Source: Derived from D.L. Kaplan and M.C. Casey, <u>Occupational Trends in the United States, 1900 to 1950</u>, Tables 6a and 6b; U.S. Bureau of the Census, <u>1960 Census of Population</u>: Vol. I, <u>Characteristics of the Population</u>, Part 1, U.S. Summary, Table 201.

of the nonfarm __nonmanual__ occupations was much greater than for the nonfarm __manual__ occupations.

As with our industry comparison, the major differences in the occupational trends between the sexes is that some of the tendencies observed for male and female workers combined seem to have started earlier for women and, in addition, to have been more pronounced for women in several cases. By 1900, for example, women were already much more concentrated than men in nonfarm occupations--81 percent of the female labor force, as compared to 58 percent of the male labor force, was in nonfarm occupations at that date (Table 5.4). We might have suspected from our comparisons of industrial distributions that this was the case, but the industry data by sex did not go farther back than 1940, so we could not be sure. Women had therefore started earlier than men to profit from the rapid expansion of job opportunities which occurred in the nonfarm sector. In addition, although the same proportion of female as male workers was in nonmanual occupations in 1900, within this category the proportion of female workers in the professions and in clerical work was much higher. Again, women had a head start, so to speak, in two groups of occupations that were to expand very rapidly in the next sixty years. Partly because of this, perhaps, the increase in the proportions in nonmanual occupations has been much greater for women than for men-- from 18 to 53 percent for women, as compared to 18 to 34 percent for men, in the 1900-1960 period.

Undoubtedly a major factor in this very rapid growth of the female labor force in nonmanual occupations has been that by 1900 women had monopolized or nearly monopolized several clerical and professional occupations that were numerically small in 1900, but which grew very rapidly in the next sixty years. Chart 5.5 gives examples of four occupations where this was the case. All are occupations in which women constituted 70 percent or more of the workers in 1900.[1] The growth of employment in these occupations (for male and female workers combined) has been nothing short of phenomenal. The four occupations combined constituted only 8.4 percent of the female labor force in 1900, but they accounted for 23.4 percent of the growth in the female labor force between 1900 and 1960. By 1960, 19.9 percent of all female workers were in these four occupations.[2]

---

[1]In 1900 women constituted 72 percent of stenographers, typists, and secretaries; 80 percent of telephone operators; 94 percent of nurses; and 75 percent of teachers (Kaplan and Casey, Tables 6 and 6b).

[2]Ibid., and U.S. Bureau of the Census, 1960 Census of Population: Vol. I, Characteristics of the Population, Part 1, U.S. Summary, Table 201.

CHART 5.5.   GROWTH OF THE LABOR FORCE IN SELECTED OCCUPATIONS:
1900-1960

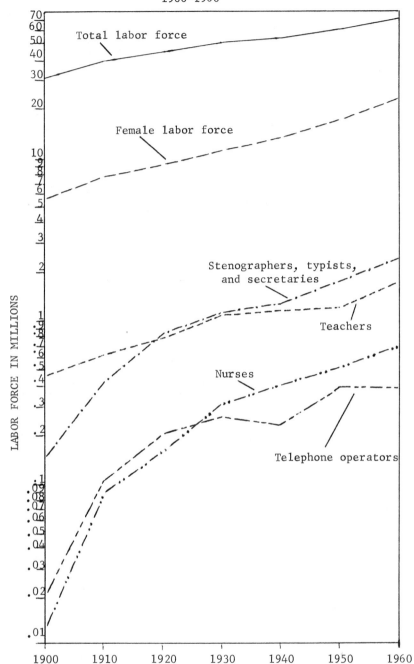

Sources: D.L. Kaplan and M.C. Casey, Occupational Trends in the
United States, 1900 to 1950, Tables 6 and 6b; U.S. Bureau of the
Census, 1960 Census of Population: Vol. I, Characteristics of
the Population, Part 1, U.S. Summary, Table 201.

Another difference between the occupational trends for men and women is that although there is evidence that, for both, the growth rate of manual occupations has not kept pace recently with that of nonmanual occupations, this is more the case for women than for men. As a consequence, while the proportion of males in nonfarm manual occupations went up slightly from 1940 to 1960 (from 51.7 to 53.3 percent), the proportion of female workers in these occupations declined from 51.1 percent in 1940 to 39.4 percent in 1960.

In general, we see that both the female and male labor forces have exhibited very similar overall occupational trends. This is somewhat surprising when we consider that men and women are not readily interchangeable in particular jobs. Nevertheless, in terms of very gross occupational divisions there is a considerable similarity in the trends for the two sexes. The major differences are that the female labor force has been the first to exhibit the long-term trends we have noted for both sexes, and that it has exhibited these trends in a more intense form. Far from being atypical, the female labor force has been as supertypical in its overall occupational trends as in its industrial trends.

There are several reasons for believing that the industrial and occupational trends we have been considering for the United States are not limited to this society but are, in many ways, characteristic of industrially developing societies in general--at the very least of those within the sphere of the European cultural experience. This is basically Colin Clark's thesis, of course.[3] Clark argues that as per capita income rises in a society, "the numbers engaged in agriculture tend to decline relative to the numbers in manufacture, which in their turn decline relative to the numbers engaged in services."[4] Clark's support for this thesis is of two kinds--statistical and theoretical. On the one hand, he cites considerable statistical evidence from many countries.[5] On the other hand, he argues that there are several cogent reasons why we should expect the industrial shifts in composition which are statistically observed. First of all, he argues that as real income per head increases, the relative demand for agricultural products falls and the relative demand for manufactured goods rises, and then falls in favor

---

[3] The Conditions of Economic Progress, 3rd ed. (London: Macmillan & Co., Ltd., 1947), Ch. IX, "The Distribution of Labour Between Industries," pp. 490-520.

[4] Ibid., p. 492.

[5] Ibid., pp. 510-520.

of services. Second, he argues that productivity in agriculture and manufacturing tends to rise faster than productivity in the service industries. As a consequence, a stationary or decreasing relative demand for manufactured goods or agricultural products (which he has posited will result as per capita income rises) will lead to a decrease in the proportion of the labor force employed in agriculture and manufacturing.[6]

For an entirely different set of reasons, Leibenstein also argues that rising per capita income will be accompanied by the industrial shifts Clark posits.[7] Leibenstein also attempts to provide reasons for the sort of general occupational shifts we have been noting in the American labor force. He divides occupations into three groups roughly parallel to the three industry groupings. However, while the industry groupings are based on the activity of the production unit, the occupational groupings are based on the activities of the individual workers composing them. Someone engaged in a primary occupation is thus engaged, among other things, in the production of commodities closest to

----

[6]Ibid., pp. 493-495. At one point Clark modifies his thesis to say that in some cases productivity may rise faster in services, but that this usually seems to be more than offset by rises in the demand for services (ibid., pp. 494-495). Bauer and Yamey have criticized Clark's thesis--particularly with regard to the relative size and growth of employment in the tertiary sector supposedly associated with economic development. They argue that in West Africa, for example, a tremendous number of people are involved in trade as a secondary occupation, a situation which apparently is not reflected in the statistics on occupation. They also argue that the relative demand for services need not increase more than the relative demand for manufactured goods. Furthermore, they maintain that the proportion engaged in the different industry groups will depend on the extent to which unpaid labor is substituted for paid labor. However, they do not present evidence that their criticisms hold for the European and American experiences (P.T. Bauer and B.S. Yamey, "Economic Progress and Occupational Distribution," The Economic Journal, LXI [December 1951], pp. 741-755). See also Richard H. Holton, "Marketing Structure and Economic Development," Quarterly Journal of Economics, LXVII (April 1953), pp. 344-361. Triantis, on the other hand, has several cogent criticisms of the Bauer and Yamey argument (S.G. Triantis, "Economic Progress, Occupational Redistribution and International Terms of Trade," The Economic Journal, LXIII [September 1953], pp. 626-637).

[7]Harvey Leibenstein, Economic Backwardness and Economic Growth (New York: John Wiley & Sons, Inc., 1957), Ch. 7, "Specialization, Income Level, and Occupational Structure," pp. 77-93.

nature. Someone engaged in secondary activities is engaged in the manipulation of primary materials into a somewhat different form. Finally, in tertiary activities, a service rather than a tangible product is involved. Farm occupations fall into the primary group, of course; nonfarm manual occupations fall into the secondary group to the extent that they are engaged in manufacturing; and nonmanual occupations fall into the tertiary group.

In general, Leibenstein's argument that certain industrial and occupational shifts accompany rising per capita income is based on his thesis that increased income implies a more elaborate division of labor--i.e., increased specialization.[8] This, in turn, necessarily leads to the hypothesized occupational and industrial shifts.[9] In the case of agriculture, for example, as specialization increases, some operations will be carried out by new production units no longer primarily engaged in agriculture. These will be of two kinds--those producing physical goods utilized in agricultural production (farm equipment and fertilizer, for example) and those producing services that are utilized by the agricultural production unit (marketing and transportation services, for example). Increased specialization in agriculture, therefore, leads to the creation of manufacturing and service industries. The people engaged in these newly created manufacturing and service industries will obviously not be in farming occupations. In the manufacturing industries, many will be in manual occupations of a skilled or semiskilled variety; in the service industries, most will be in nonmanual occupations.

Increased specialization within the manufacturing sector will lead, as with agriculture, to the creation of service production units. The argument is basically that increased specialization narrows the range of activities per man, and hence some men cease to spend time transforming raw materials. To the extent such activities are coordinated in independent production units, tertiary industries are created. Whether or not independent tertiary industries are created, there will be an increase in the proportion who are engaged in tertiary, rather than secondary, activities, i.e., service and nonmanual occupations. This reasoning can also be applied to specialization within the agricultural sector. With increased specialization some people employed by agricultural production units, and hence in the primary industry category, will not be engaged in primary, but rather tertiary, activities--bookkeeping, for example.

A significant aspect of these industrial and occupational shifts is that although increased specialization in primary

---

[8]Ibid., pp. 82ff.

[9]Ibid., pp. 91-93.

industries leads to the creation of secondary industries, the reverse is not true. There is no shift from manufacturing to primary type industries with increased specialization, since "primary types of activities are not performed to any extent by secondary industry."[10] Similarly, tertiary industries cannot lose to the other two industry groups as a consequence of increased specialization.

In sum, Leibenstein concludes that on the basis of the specialization-income relationship, we are able to get some confirmation of Clark's thesis.[11] In addition, he provides us with reasons for the decline in employment in farm occupations, and the rapid growth in manual and nonmanual occupations. Increased specialization within primary industries increases the proportion of workers within these industries who are not engaged in primary activities, and it also leads to the creation of secondary and tertiary production units in which the workers are not engaged in primary economic activities. Increased specialization within secondary industries never leads to the creation of primary activities or production units, but does lead to the creation of tertiary production units and occupations solely concerned with tertiary rather than secondary activities. Finally, increased specialization within the tertiary industry group leads to the proliferation of both tertiary occupations and industries.

Implications of Industrial and Occupational Shifts

We have seen that there are several theoretical as well as statistical reasons why the overall industrial and occupational trends experienced in the United States can be thought of as characteristic of industrially developing societies in general. These industrial and occupational shifts have important implications for the central concern of this monograph--namely, accounting for changes in female labor force participation. If shifts in the industrial and occupational composition of the labor force are to be expected in a developing economy, then these shifts can all be restated in terms of shifts in the demand for labor rather than shifts in the supply of labor. If there are changes in industrial and occupational composition because of increases in the relative demand for manufactured goods and for services, because of differentials in productivity among industry sectors, and because of increased specialization, then all these changes imply changes in the composition of the demand for labor, if not also increases in the amount of labor demanded. They do not imply

---

[10]Ibid., p. 92.

[11]Ibid.

changes in the <u>supply</u> of labor, except to the extent that increases or shifts in demand stimulate a responding increase or shift in the amount and type of labor supplied.

The industrial and occupational changes that seem to be characteristic of a developing economy (and have clearly characterized the economy of the United States) have all favored women as much as, if indeed not more than, men. This is because the increases in labor demand have been greatest in industries and occupations that have for some time been important employers of women. These increases in the demand for workers in certain occupations and industries can legitimately be translated into an increase in the demand for <u>female</u> labor because, as we have seen in Chapter 3, jobs tend to acquire sex labels and, as a consequence, the demands for workers tend to be sex-specific.

We can get some idea of the trend in the demand for female labor by utilizing the analysis of male and female labor markets undertaken in Chapter 3. We shall use the number of women in occupations where 70 percent or more of the workers are female as an estimate of the demand for female workers. It is highly unlikely that the number of female workers in such "female occupations" will overestimate the demand for female labor. As we saw in Chapter 3, it will probably <u>underestimate</u> this demand. For one thing, the coarser the occupational classification system, the more likely it is that two or more occupations, each employing only one sex, will be combined and appear as a mixed sex category. (Unfortunately, there is little that can be done about this problem.)

A second reason why these data can be expected to <u>under</u>estimate the number of women in female jobs is that industry, as well as occupations, delimits labor markets. As we saw for 1960, when we cross-classified only a few general occupational categories by industry, the proportion of women in occupation-industry combinations where 70 percent or more of the workers were women was increased by almost one-fifth.[12] In an effort to make allowance for this industry factor, we shall increase our initial estimate of the demand for female labor, based on occupational concentrations alone, by one-fifth for every census year under consideration. This adjustment for the industry effect is quite conservative, for a cross-classification of <u>all</u> occupations by detailed industry (not merely five occupations) undoubtedly would have increased still further the proportion of women in occupation-industry combinations where at least 70 percent of the workers were female.

---

[12]See Chapter 3, pp. 72-75 above.

Table 5.5 shows the trend in the demand for female labor as indicated by our estimates. As expected, the demand has been rising throughout the 1900-1960 period. The increase was particularly sharp in the 1950-1960 period, when there was about a 40 percent rise in the demand for female workers. It should be pointed out, however, that our estimates may somewhat exaggerate the rise in demand. This is because, on the whole, the occupational classification system has become more detailed, which tends to increase the number of female occupations that can be distinguished.

Table 5.5

DEMAND FOR FEMALE LABOR, ESTIMATED ON THE BASIS OF THE NUMBER
OF WOMEN IN FEMALE OCCUPATIONS:
1900-1960[a]

	1900	1920	1930	1940	1950	1960
Number (in thousands)	2,607	3,935	5,727	7,278	8,819	12,382
Percent increase	--	50.9[b]	45.5	27.1	21.2	40.4

[a]"Female occupations" are those where 70 percent or more of the workers were female. The number of women in such occupations was increased by one-fifth to allow for the industry factor in the segregation of male and female labor markets.

[b]This change is for a twenty-year period; all the other figures refer to ten-year periods.

Source: Derived from D.L. Kaplan and M.C. Casey, Occupational Trends in the United States, 1900 to 1950, Bureau of the Census Working Paper No. 5 (Washington, 1958), Tables 6 and 6b; U.S. Bureau of the Census, 1960 Census of Population: Vol. I, Characteristics of the Population, Part 1, U.S. Summary, Table 201; 1960 Census of Population: Subject Report PC(2)-7C, Occupation by Industry, Table 2.

In using these estimates we cannot tell, of course, the extent to which the increase in demand has been due to the expansion of traditionally female occupations, the growth of new female occupations, or the extensive substitution of women for men. All that is measured is growth in occupations where 70 percent or more of the workers are women; these may not be the

same occupations at every census date.[13] Unfortunately, the data
are not sufficiently comparable for the entire period to trace
the growth of particular occupations. However, for the 1950-1960
period we can get some idea of what share of the growth in female
employment can be attributed to the growth of occupations which
were predominantly female in 1950.

In Table 5.6 we see that for the major occupational groups
in which women are an important component, the growth of employment in female occupations accounted for a substantial proportion
of the net growth in the occupational group. Among clerical and
kindred workers, for example, about 66 percent of the net growth
in female employment for the group as a whole was in clerical occupations where 70 percent or more of the workers were women in
1950. If we calculate the proportion of the net growth in employment which was in occupations where 50 percent or more of the
workers were women, the results are even more impressive. In the
case of service workers, as high as 94 percent of the growth in
female employment for the group as a whole was in those service
occupations where women were in the majority. On the whole, about
48 percent of the total net increase in the number of employed females between 1950 and 1960 was in occupations where women were
at least 70 percent of the workers; 59 percent was in occupations
where women were in the majority.[14]

The crudity of our data limits these estimates severely;
a fairly high proportion of employed females--in 1960 especially--
are classified in groups that are very vaguely defined. For example, over 8 percent of employed females in 1960 were in the
"Clerical and kindred worker (n.e.c.)" category, 7 percent were
in the "Salesmen and sales clerks (n.e.c.)" category, and almost
6 percent did not have their occupations reported at all. As a
result, about 32 percent of the net growth between 1950 and 1960
was in these "residual" categories.[15] In other words, only about
68 percent of the net growth in female employment occurred in
occupational categories that lent themselves to a meaningful

---

[13]However, as we saw in Table 3.5, there is considerable
continuity with respect to which occupations are predominantly
female.

[14]For a somewhat similar analysis with similar results, see
Dale L. Hiestand, _Economic Growth and Employment Opportunities
for Minorities_ (New York: Columbia University Press, 1964),
pp. 30-35.

[15]U.S. Bureau of the Census, _1960 Census of Population:_ Vol.
I, _Characteristics of the Population,_ Part 1, U.S. Summary,
Table 202.

THE FEMALE LABOR FORCE IN THE UNITED STATES

Table 5.6

NET GROWTH IN FEMALE EMPLOYMENT ATTRIBUTABLE TO GROWTH IN
OCCUPATIONS WHERE AT LEAST 50-70 PERCENT OF THE
WORKERS WERE FEMALES IN 1950:
1950-1960

| | Percent of total net growth due to net growth in occupations: | |
	50 percent or more female in 1950	70 percent or more female in 1950
Total employed females	59.2	47.5
Professional, technical and kindred workers	65.8	54.4
Clerical and kindred workers	66.1	66.1
Operatives	66.6	29.3
Private household workers	100.0	100.0
Other service workers	93.7	44.2

Source: Derived from U.S. Bureau of the Census, 1960 Census of Population: Vol. I, Characteristics of the Population, Part 1, U.S. Summary, Table 202.

analysis of sex composition. When viewed in this light, the share of total growth which was in occupations where 50-70 percent or more of the workers were women is even more amazing.

In sum, we have seen that there is substantial evidence that the demand for female labor has been increasing over the years. Furthermore, this rising demand can to a large extent be attributed to a rise in the demand for workers in typically female occupations--clerical work and several occupations in the professional and service categories. On the whole, this suggests that perhaps the best explanation for the overall increase in female labor force participation in recent years is that there has been an increase in the demand for female workers which has, in turn, stimulated an increase in the supply of women to the labor market. Factors such as household labor-saving devices, which may operate to increase the supply of female labor independently of the stimulus of demand, have facilitated the entry of women into the labor market, but there is little evidence that they were precipitating factors in the situation.

160

Whether the increase in the demand for female labor is the most satisfactory explanation for the rising female work rate depends, however, on whether the supply of females to the labor force is responsive to demand. The fact that according to our estimates both demand and the female labor force have been rising suggests that the female labor supply _is_ responsive to demand. This conclusion is bolstered by the fact that we have been unable to discover supply factors operating independently of demand which, on their own, can provide a satisfactory explanation of the increase in female labor force participation. Furthermore, as we have seen, there is considerable evidence that a variety of factors have been operating--quite independently of supply-- to increase the demand for female labor. Unfortunately, all this is indirect rather than direct evidence for the argument that the supply of female labor is responsive to demand. Recent studies on the correlates of the female work rate provide some additional material on the point, however.

In a regression analysis utilizing annual data for the 1948-1962 period, Alfred Tella has found that short-term variations in labor supply were closely correlated with variations in demand, as measured by employment.[16] Of special interest is Tella's finding that the female labor force in particular was responsive to changing job opportunities. In general he found that

> in period of slack employment, females reveal a greater
> tendency to leave and/or not to enter the labor force,
> while males show more of a tendency to continue to
> enter and/or to remain in the labor force. In periods
> of rising employment, females become attracted into
> the labor force more rapidly and/or leave less rapidly
> than males.[17]

Another study relevant to this question is Bowen and Finegan's multiple regression analysis of the relationship between the labor force (supply) and several other variables.[18] This is

---

[16]"The Relation of Labor Force to Employment," _Industrial and Labor Relations Review_ (April 1964), pp. 454-469.

[17]_Ibid._, p. 455. Tella found that the correlation between female labor force participation rates and the ratio of employment to population was $r = 0.97$ (_ibid._, p. 459).

[18]William G. Bowen and T.A. Finegan, "Labor Force Participation and Unemployment," in Arthur M. Ross, ed., _Employment Policy and the Labor Market_ (Berkeley: University of California Press, 1965), pp. 115-161.

not a time series analysis, but a cross-sectional analysis using data for Standard Metropolitan Statistical Areas at three census dates--1940, 1950, and 1960. Of special interest are their findings on the effect of labor-market conditions, the demand for female labor, and the supply of women on the labor force participation of married women with husbands present. Bowen and Finegan's estimate of the demand for female labor was constructed by assigning to a city "a higher value according to the greater concentration of employment in that city in industries which on a nationwide basis have a relatively high percentage of female employment."[19] For example, on a national basis, service industries tend to be large employers of women. A city with a high proportion of the labor force in services--Washington, D.C., for example--will therefore presumably have a high demand for female workers. On the other hand, a city whose economy is based mainly on heavy industry will have relatively few job opportunities for women. In general, Bowen and Finegan found a strong _positive_ relationship in all three census years between their estimate of the demand for female labor and the labor force participation of married women. They also found an equally strong _negative_ relationship between the overall unemployment rate and the labor force participation of married women.[20] All this supports the thesis that the supply of married women is responsive to demand.

Another interesting finding of the study is that the labor force rate of married women was negatively correlated with the supply of all women aged 14 or older in a city.[21] This finding is consistent with the idea that the demand for married women is related to the supply of women--when that supply is low, greater job opportunities exist for married women, and they respond by entering the labor force.

In general, then, Tella's study provides evidence that short-run variations in the female labor force seem to be responsive to variations in demand. The Bowen and Finegan study shows that, at three census dates at least, the work rate of married women in SMSA's is correlated with unemployment, the demand for female labor, and the overall supply of females. This too is evidence of the responsiveness of labor supply to labor demand.[22]

---

[19]_Ibid._, p. 135.

[20]_Ibid._, pp. 136-137.

[21]_Ibid._

[22]Bancroft reports on a multiple regression analysis by Lebergott in which he found that "the equation that gave the most satisfactory account of short-term variations in the participation rate

Comparison of Demand Estimates and Supply Estimates

As we have seen, there are good reasons for believing that a major, if not the major, precipitating factor in the overall increase in female labor force participation in the 1940-1960 period was an increase in the demand for female labor. However, the most dramatic change during these years was not the increase in the work rate for all women combined, but for married and older women. As a consequence, the whole family-cycle pattern of female labor force participation has undergone a radical change. How can we account for this change? The fact that there has been an increase in the demand for female workers in general is not in itself an adequate explanation of the great shifts in the age-specific rates. The rise in the work rate for older women was so much larger than the rise in the overall work rate that it suggests that something more complex than a simple rise in demand was involved. If, however, we compare the trends in the demand for female labor with the trends in the growth of the population groups which have traditionally been the major suppliers of female labor, it becomes obvious that the only way the demand for females could have been met was by employing older married women. Thus, while demand alone seems to have been the major factor determining the rise in the total work rate, the explanation for the much larger increases for older women appears to lie in the interaction of demand with the supply of potential workers.

Our next task, then, is to compare trends in the demand for female labor with trends in the supply of women in various population groups. Since any estimates of demand or supply are, of necessity, quite rough, the best procedure is to construct a variety of estimates of supply and demand according to a range of assumptions, so as to avoid putting too much weight on any one set of estimates. We shall therefore construct three series of demand estimates and six series of supply estimates, and then compare them.

Estimates of the Demand for Female Workers

Employed Females as the Estimate of Demand. Probably one of the most liberal estimates of the demand for female workers at

---

of adult women was one that combined measures reflecting job opportunities for women on the one hand, and male unemployment on the other" (Gertrude Bancroft, "Labor Force Growth and Job Opportunities: Some Doctrines and the Evidence," Exploring the Dimensions of the Manpower Revolution, Vol. 1 of Selected Readings in Employment and Manpower, U.S. Senate, Committee on Labor and Public Welfare, Subcommittee on Employment and Manpower, 88th Congress, 2nd Session, Washington: U.S. Government Printing Office, 1964).

163

any given date is the number of women actually employed at that date. In effect, such an estimate assumes that there is practically no interchangeability of male and female labor, so that every job in which a female happens to be employed has a feminine sex label attached to it. This estimate of demand has the deficiency of not including demands for female labor that are not filled. In this respect it underestimates the demand for female labor to an unknown degree.

There is a problem in constructing an estimate of demand based on employment, because we do not have data available on the number of employed females in the 1900-1930 period. However, we have estimates of the female labor force during that period, and Lebergott has constructed estimates of total employment and unemployment going back to 1900.[23] We can therefore arrive at a rough estimate of female employment for 1900-1930 by assuming that the percentage of the female labor force which was employed was the same as Lebergott's estimate of the percentage of the total labor force which was employed. Our first estimate of demand at every census date, then, will be the estimated number of females employed at these dates.

The Number of Females in Female Occupations as the Estimate of Demand. Our second estimate of the demand for female labor is the estimate utilized in the first part of this chapter--namely, the adjusted number of women in occupations where at least 70 percent of the workers were women. It is an effort to be more realistic than the estimate based on female employment can claim to be. However, as we have already emphasized, estimates of the number of women in female occupations is a very conservative estimate of demand, because the data are crude.[24]

Employment in 1900 as the Estimate of Demand. Our third series of estimates uses as its basis our estimate of the

---

[23]Lebergott, p. 519.

[24]This estimate of demand is somewhat inflated compared to the other estimates, however, because it was impossible to eliminate from the occupational data females 10-17 years old for 1900-1930, 14-17 years old for 1940-1960, and 65 years old and over for the 1900-1960 period as a whole. The other two estimates of demand are based on work rates for females 18-64 years old only. The difference between the size of the female labor force 18-64 years old and the female labor force the occupational data are based upon (females 10 years old and over for 1900-1930 and 14 years old and over for 1940-1960) ranges from a minimum of about 400,000 in 1930 to a maximum of 1.7 million in 1960. On the whole, the difference is in the neighborhood of one million for most census dates (Table 5.7 below; Kaplan and Casey, Table 6b; 1960 Census of Population, Characteristics, Table 201).

proportion of women employed in 1900. For the early part of the century, this undoubtedly yields an overestimate of the demand for female workers, because it is identical with the first series of estimates of demand for 1900, and fairly close to the 1920 estimates in this series. However, it greatly underestimates the demand in the 1940-1960 period, and is used primarily to provide a very conservative estimate of the demand for female labor in the more recent period. This third series of the estimate of the demand for female labor, then, applies the estimated proportion of women 18-64 years old who were employed in 1900 to the number of women 18-64 years old in the other census dates under consideration.

In sum, we have three series of estimates of the demand for female labor in the 1900-1960 period. The first provides a maximum estimate, because it is based on the number of employed females at each census date. The third provides what is probably a minimum estimate for the most recent dates, because it uses the estimated proportion of females who were employed in 1900 as the estimate of demand in all the census years. The second is an effort to provide a fairly realistic estimate, by counting only women in predominantly female occupations. However, because of the generality of the occupational classification system, as well as other important factors, such as the influence of industry, which are difficult to take into account, this second series is probably an underestimate of demand.

The three series of demand estimates are given in Table 5.7 and Chart 5.6. The range in the estimates is quite large. In 1960, for example, the minimum estimate of the demand for female labor was 9.8 million, while the maximum was 19.5 million. Such a wide range in variation between the two extremes will not, however, seriously affect our comparisons with estimates of the supply of female labor.

Estimates of the Supply of Potential Female Workers

As we saw in Chapter 1, the typical female worker in 1900 was young and single. By 1940 the female labor force, as well as the female population, had aged somewhat, and in addition, a growing proportion were widowed, divorced, or separated. Nevertheless, in 1940, 59 percent of all female workers were still under 35 years old, and 49 percent were single (as compared to 48 percent under 35 years old and 28 percent single in the female population as a whole). As high as 70 percent were single, widowed, divorced, or married with husbands absent.[25] The typical

---

[25]See Table 1.9 in Chapter 1 above.

Table 5.7

VARIOUS ESTIMATES OF THE DEMAND FOR FEMALE WORKERS:
1900-1960

(in thousands)

Estimates of demand	1900	1920	1930	1940	1950	1960
Demand estimated on the basis of the proportion of females 18-64 years old who were employed in 1900[a]	3,965	5,813	7,024	8,018	9,051	9,815
Demand estimated on the basis of the number of women in female occupations[b]	2,607	3,935	5,727	7,278	8,819	12,382
Demand equated with the size of the employed female population 18-64 years old[a]	3,965	6,997	8,884	10,782	14,849	19,517

[a]The employed female population in the 1900-1930 period was estimated on the basis of Lebergott's estimates of total employment in these years.

[b]Female occupations are those where 70 percent or more of the workers were female. The number of women in such occupations was increased by one-fifth to allow for the industry factor in the segregation of male and female labor markets. The occupational data this demand estimate is based on include all women 10 years old and older for 1900-1930, and 14 years old and older for 1940-1960.

Source: Table 3.4 in Chapter 3 above; Stanley Lebergott, Man-power in Economic Growth (New York: McGraw-Hill Book Co., 1964), p. 512; D. Kaplan and C. Casey, Occupational Trends in the United States, 1900 to 1950, Bureau of the Census Working Paper No. 5, Tables 6 and 6b; Gertrude Bancroft, The American Labor Force (New York: John Wiley & Sons, Inc., 1958), Table D-1; U.S. Bureau of the Census, 1940 Census of Population: Vol. III, The Labor Force, Table 8; 1960 Census of Population: Vol. I, Characteristics of the Population, Part 1, U.S. Summary, Tables 195 and 201.

CHART 5.6. THREE ESTIMATES OF THE DEMAND FOR FEMALE LABOR:
1920-1960

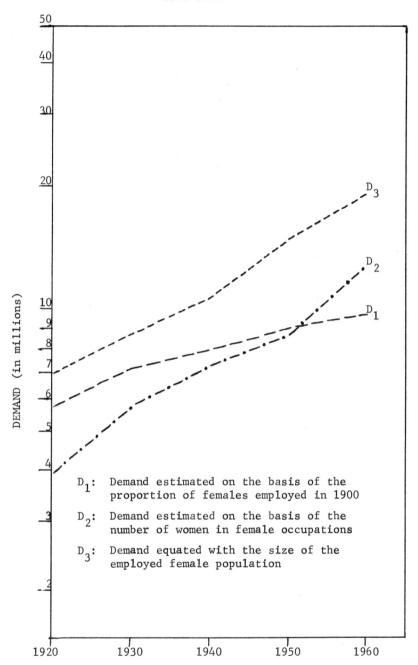

D₁: Demand estimated on the basis of the proportion of females employed in 1900

D₂: Demand estimated on the basis of the number of women in female occupations

D₃: Demand equated with the size of the employed female population

Source: Table 5.7.

female worker in 1940, therefore, was not a married woman living
with her husband. We know that by 1960, however, the typical female worker was married and living with her husband--55.1 percent,
in fact.[26] We shall attempt to determine whether this increasing
reliance on married women has been due to a growing divergence
between the demand for female workers and the supply of young
single women and other women without husbands to support them.
This divergence in supply and demand must have become particularly
acute since 1940, if this hypothesis has any merit. We shall begin by constructing six pools of women which will represent sources
of the supply of various types of female labor.

Single Women 18-34 Years Old. The first pool consists
of all single women 18-34 years old, with the exception of girls
18-19 years old who were enrolled in school. The deduction of
those enrolled in school is made for this pool (and all the others
as well) in order to make some allowance for the withdrawal of
girls from the labor market because of school attendance. Women
20 years old or over who were enrolled in school were not deducted,
because of the dual status often encountered among them. This
pool was set up to correspond, first of all, with employer preferences for young single women, as expressed in studies of the
1940's. It is also an estimate of the supply of the type of female worker typical around the turn of the century.

Employers may simply have preferred youth, and cared
little about the marital or family status of their female employees, except perhaps during depressions. However, a very high
proportion of married women 18-34 years old who had husbands present also had young children, and so were unavailable for employment outside the home. The young women who most likely would have
been available for labor force participation throughout the 1900-
1960 period were, therefore, single women and ever-married women
who, through one circumstance or another (widowhood, divorce,
desertion, etc.), did not have husbands present. The following
two pools were defined to correspond to this group.

Women 18-34 Years Old, Except for Married Women with
Husbands Present. In part, this pool constitutes an effort to
measure the supply of the more typical worker of the early 1940's--
the young unmarried woman, or married woman not living with her
husband. More important, the pool is an effort to measure the
supply of young women preferred by employers in the 1940's, de-
ducting those less likely to have been available for labor force
participation in 1940--namely married women living with their
husbands.

---

[26] Ibid.

Women 18-34 Years Old, Except for Married Women with
Husbands Present and Pre-school-age Children. The third pool is
the last effort to measure the supply of young women. Only married women who were living with their husbands and who, in addition, had pre-school-age children were excluded. These excluded
women were a group which, even in 1960, had much lower work rates
than women at any other point in the family life cycle. In 1940,
very few of them were employed. This pool probably provides a
very good estimate of the maximum supply of young women that
could have been available at any date. It is thus a good test
of the practicality of employer preferences for young women. It
is true, of course, that some married women with husbands present
and with pre-school-age children have always been available for
employment. However, the number has been relatively small, and
has likely been more than offset by those among the other young
women--single, widowed, divorced, and married with husbands ab-
sent--who have not been available for employment, but are included
in the pool.

Single, Widowed, and Divorced Women 18-64 Years Old.
The fourth pool is a fairly good approximation of the typical female worker of 1940. It is composed of those women least likely
to have had men to support them; it does not include married
women whose husbands could not or would not provide adequate support. In an effort to estimate these, data for the 1940-1960
period giving information on the presence of husbands were used
to construct a fifth pool.

Women 18-64 Years Old, Except for Married Women with
Husbands Present. The fifth pool gives an estimate of the supply
of all women 18-64 years old, with the exception of women who
were married and living with their husbands. It is an effort to
measure the supply of the type of female worker most characteristic
of 1940, when 70 percent of the female labor force consisted of
such women.

Women 18-64 Years Old, Except for Married Women with
Husbands Present and Pre-School-age Children. The sixth and
last pool forms the maximum estimate of the supply of potential
female workers. It includes all women except those who were
least likely to have been employed, even in 1960, and who were
most likely to have met the greatest opposition to employment
from family norms regarding the care of young children.

All these estimates of the supply of female workers are
only estimates of the supply of potential female workers, because
little effort has been made--or can be made--to deduct the number
of women in the pools who would have been unavailable for employment. For example, no effort has been made to account for the
widowed, divorced, or married women (husbands absent) who had a
regular income, and some of whom, at least, had no desire to work.

This was particularly likely to be the case if they had young
children. In 1960, although a higher proportion of these women
worked than did married women living with their husbands, the
proportion was well below 70 percent for most age groups.[27] A
general idea of the extent to which the women in each of the
pools participated in the labor force is given in Table 5.8.[28]

Table 5.8

WORK RATES OF VARIOUS GROUPS OF WOMEN:
1940 AND 1960

	1940	1960
Women 18-34 years old		
Single	67.0	67.0
Unmarried and married with husband absent	66.2	64.4
Unmarried, married (husband absent), and married (husband present) with no pre-school-age children[a]	49.5	59.4
Women 18-64 years old		
Unmarried and married with husband absent	59.0	63.6
Unmarried, married (husband absent), and married (husband present) with no pre-school-age children[a]	34.3	48.7

[a]Children under five in 1940; under six in 1960.

Sources: Derived from U.S. Bureau of the Census, 1940 Census of
Population: The Labor Force (Sample Statistics), Employment and
Family Characteristics of Women, Tables 1 and 2; 1960 Census of
Population: Subject Report No. PC(2)-6A, Employment Status and
Work Experience, Table 6; Subject Report No. PC(2)-5B, Education-
al Attainment, Table 5.

[27]See Table 1.4 in Chapter 1 above.

[28]The figures in Table 5.8 do not exactly measure the proportions
of the women in each pool in the labor force, because no allowance
was made for the girls 18-19 years old enrolled in school who were
deducted from the pools. In addition, the proportions working in
one of the pools--single, widowed, and divorced women 18-64 years
old--were omitted due to lack of data.

It is evident that the proportion of women working in each of the pools was well below the maximum. Even among single women 18-34 years old--the group with the highest work rates--only 67 percent were in the labor force in 1960. Furthermore, except for the pools including married women (husband present) with no pre-school-age children, there was not much of a change in the proportions in the labor force in the 1940-1960 period. Therefore, while the women in the six pools have a much higher propensity to work than other women in the population, we cannot assume that all of these women can be drawn into the labor force.

In general, then, all six of the pools of potential female workers which we have set up overestimate the number of such women available for labor force participation. However, since we are trying to determine whether shortages in the supply of various types of female labor have been developing, overestimates of supply should lead to a rather conservative analysis.

Trends in Supply. Table 5.9 and Charts 5.7 and 5.8 show the trend in the supply of female workers as defined by the six pools. Although the female population as a whole has been growing, and this growth has accelerated since 1940, and although the supply of young women--as defined by the first three pools--increased in the 1900-1940 period, the supply of young women has been declining since 1940. The decline in the number of single women 18-34 years old has been particularly great--a decrease of 2.8 million, or 46 percent, between 1940 and 1960. Thus, in a period when the demand for female labor has been rising, the supply of young women--those who would be most eligible for employment--has been declining sharply. On the whole, the supply of women in the three pools in the 18-64 age group has also been declining in the 1940-1960 period. Only the pool of women 18-64 years old exclusive of those married with husbands present and with pre-school-age children exhibited a slight increase in that period. In general, in the 1900-1940 period, both supply and demand were increasing. However, in the critical 1940-1960 period--when the whole pattern of female labor force participation underwent enormous changes--demand continued to rise, but the supply declined.

The main reasons why these pools have been shifting in size--a shift sometimes at variance with the overall population trends--are (1) declines in the age at marriage and the proportion never marrying, (2) the aging of the population, (3) postwar rises in fertility, and (4) increases in school enrollments.

As we can see from Table 5.10, there has been a long-run decline in the age at marriage which became very sharp after 1940. Over 50 percent of women 20-24 years old were single in 1900; the proportion had declined only slightly by 1940 (to 47.2 percent), but by 1960 only 28.4 percent of young women in this age

Table 5.9

POOLS OF POTENTIAL FEMALE WORKERS:
1900-1960

(in thousands)

Pools[a]	1900	1920	1930	1940	1950	1960
(1) Single women 18-34	4,131	4,880	5,407	6,114	4,148	3,284
(2) Women 18-34, unmarried[b] and married with husbands absent	--c	--c	--c	7,236	5,564	4,853
(3) Women 18-34, except for married women (husband present) with pre-school-age children[d]	--c	--c	--c	13,037	12,160[e]	8,950
(4) Single, widowed, and divorced women 18-64	6,884	9,107	10,578	12,101	10,741	10,311
(5) Women 18-64, unmarried[b] and married with husbands absent	--c	--c	--c	13,552	12,556	12,565
(6) Women 18-64, except for married women (husbands present) with pre-school-age children	--c	--c	--c	33,141	36,183[f]	36,133

[a]Girls 18-19 years old enrolled in school were omitted from all six pools.

[b]Includes single, widowed, and divorced.

[c]Not available.

[d]Children under five in 1940 and 1950; under six in 1960.

[e]Only women married once with pre-school-age children were excluded.

[f]Only women 18-49, married once, and with children under five excluded. It was assumed that no women 50-64 had children under five.

Sources: Derived from U.S. Bureau of the Census, 1940 Census of Population: The Labor Force (Sample Statistics), Employment and Family Characteristics of Women, Tables 1 and 4; 1950 Census of Population: Vol. II, Characteristics of the Population, Part 1, U.S. Summary, Table 110, Vol. IV, Special Reports, Part 5, Chapter C, Fertility, Tables 1, 8, 9, 10, 11, and 35; 1960 Census of Population: Vol. I, Characteristics of the Population, Part 1, U.S. Summary, Tables 166, 177, 178, and 179, Subject Report PC(2)-5B, Educational Attainment, Table 5.

CHART 5.7. POOLS OF WOMEN 18-34 YEARS OLD: 1920-1960[a]

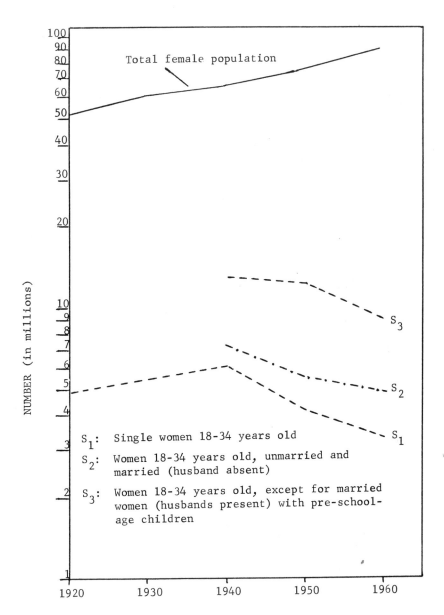

[a]Excludes girls 18-19 years old enrolled in school.

Sources: Table 5.9; U.S. Bureau of the Census, 1960 Census of Population: Vol. I, Characteristics of the Population, Part 1, U.S. Summary, Table 47.

CHART 5.8. POOLS OF WOMEN 18-64 YEARS OLD: 1920-1960[a]

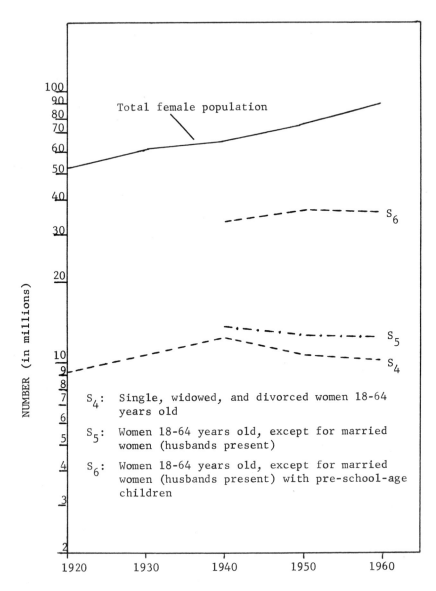

^{a}Excludes girls 18-19 years old enrolled in school.

Sources: Table 5.9; U.S. Bureau of the Census, 1960 Census of Population: Vol. I, Characteristics of the Population, Part 1, U.S. Summary, Table 47.

Table 5.10

PERCENTAGE OF WOMEN 20-24 AND 35-44 YEARS OLD WHO WERE SINGLE:
1900-1960

Age in years	1900	1920	1930	1940	1950	1960
20-24	51.6	45.6	46.0	47.2	32.3	28.4
35-44	11.1	11.4	10.0	10.4	8.3	6.1

Source: Derived from U.S. Bureau of the Census, 1960 Census of
Population: Vol. I, Characteristics of the Population, Part 1,
U.S. Summary, Table 177.

group were single.[29] Not only had the age at marriage fallen
rapidly, but the proportion of women never marrying had decreased--
from about 11 percent of women 35-44 in 1900 to 6.1 percent in
1960.

The effect on the six supply pools of these changes in
age-at-marriage and the proportion never marrying is not hard to
figure out. They obviously decreased the number of single women
in the pools, and because of the magnitude of the changes, were
a major factor in the declines of most of the pools.

One consequence of the long-run decline in fertility in
the United States was an aging of the population (Table 5.11).
In addition, the especially low Depression fertility led to cohorts which were particularly small relative to earlier cohorts.
Thus, women born in the 1930's were in their twenties in the
1950's and 1960's--the age groups where some of the highest work
rates have always occurred. As a consequence, the number of
women in the six pools we constructed--particularly the pools of
women 18-34 years old--came from a relatively diminishing segment
of the total population. The female population as a whole was
of course rising rapidly in the 1940-1960 period (see Chart 5.7).
This, however, was because of the upsurge in fertility in the
1940's.

In sum, as a consequence of the fertility trends, the
proportion of the female population under 10 years old declined
greatly between 1900 and 1940, but then rose rapidly between 1940

---

[29] The reader is reminded that according to census usage the
term "single" means never married.

Table 5.11

PERCENTAGE OF FEMALE POPULATION IN SELECTED AGE GROUPS:
1900-1960

Percentage of female population:	1900	1920	1930	1940	1950	1960
Under 10 years old	24.1	22.0	19.6	15.9	19.0	21.0
35 years old and over	29.1	33.1	36.2	40.4	43.0	43.8
65 years old and over	4.1	4.7	5.5	7.0	8.6	9.8
18-34 years old	30.1	29.3	28.8	29.3	26.6	21.5
18-64 years old	55.1	57.7	59.5	62.7	61.0	55.5

Source: Derived from U.S. Bureau of the Census, 1960 Census of
Population: Vol. I, Characteristics of the Population, Part 1,
U.S. Summary, Table 160.

and 1960. In addition, the proportion of the female population
65 years old and over was increasing throughout the 1900-1960
period. The rise in the proportion of the population 35 years
old and over was particularly great. On the whole, then, the
proportion (and sometimes even the number) of women in the age
group 18-34 was declining in the 1900-1960 period. Between 1900
and 1940 the decline was not very noteworthy, but between 1940
and 1960 the proportion of women 18-34 years old declined from
29.3 percent to 21.5 percent. This was another major factor in
the decreasing size of the pools.

Another consequence of the aging of the population is
that an increasingly higher proportion of women were in the age
groups where they were most likely to be married, and hence not
to be included in several of the pools. This was still another
factor in the decline of the pools.

Another effect of the fertility increases in the 1940's
was to increase the proportion of women who had pre-school-age
children--a group not included in any of our pools, if the women
were married and living with their husbands. Such fertility increases, therefore, operated to reduce the size of the pools.

Finally, as we can see from Table 5.12, the proportion of
18-19-year-old girls enrolled in school has been rising sharply.
This too operated to cut into the pools, since these girls were
deducted from all of them.

Table 5.12

FEMALES 18 AND 19 YEARS OLD ENROLLED IN SCHOOL:
1920-1960

| Age | Percentage of age group enrolled in school | | | | |
	1920	1930	1940	1950	1960
18 years old	22.8	30.3	34.7	37.2	46.5
19 years old	13.6	18.8	18.7	21.8	28.4

Source: U.S. Bureau of the Census, 1960 Census of Population: Vol. I, Characteristics of the Population, Part 1, U.S. Summary, Table 166.

In general, then, most of the demographic changes we have been describing operated to reduce the growth in the pools--so much so in the post-1940 period that five of the six pools declined in number.

Comparison of Trends in Demand and Supply

We have seen that the supply of potential female workers has been declining in the postwar period, while the demand for female labor has continued to rise. However, whether these divergent trends in supply and demand led to shortages of female labor depends on the relationship of supply to demand, not just the overall directions of change. The next step, then, is to compare the trends in the sizes of various pools of potential female workers with the three estimates of the demand for female workers.

The Demand for Female Labor and the Supply of Young Women. Around the turn of the century, the supply of young single women was large enough to provide the majority of female workers--even if a substantial proportion did not work. In fact, the supply was considerably larger than one of the estimates of demand (Table 5.13 and Chart 5.9). However, it has become progressively more difficult to rely on young single women to provide the backbone of the female labor force in the United States. It is true that their numbers increased in the 1900-1940 period, but this increase did not keep pace with the rate of increase of any of the three demand estimates. Furthermore, as we have seen, the number of young single women has declined sharply since 1940.

Table 5.13

ESTIMATES OF THE SUPPLY OF YOUNG WOMEN COMPARED TO ESTIMATES OF THE DEMAND FOR FEMALE WORKERS:
1900-1960

(Ratio of demand to supply)

	1900	1920	1930	1940	1950	1960
Single women 18-34 years old[a] as compared to:						
Demand estimated on the basis of the proportion of females employed in 1900	0.96	1.19	1.30	1.31	2.18	2.99
Demand estimated on the basis of the number of females in female occupations	0.63	0.81	1.06	1.19	2.13	3.77
Demand equated with the employed female population	0.96	1.43	1.64	1.76	3.58	5.94
Women 18-34 years old, unmarried or married with husbands absent[a] as compared to:						
Demand estimated on the basis of the proportion of females employed in 1900	--	--	--	1.11	1.63	2.02
Demand estimated on the basis of the number of females in female occupations	--	--	--	1.00	1.58	2.55
Demand equated with the employed female population	--	--	--	1.49	2.67	4.02
Women 18-34 years old, except for married women (husbands present) with pre-school-age children[a] as compared to:						
Demand estimated on the basis of the proportion of females employed in 1900	--	--	--	0.62	0.74	1.10
Demand estimated on the basis of the number of females in female occupations	--	--	--	0.56	0.72	1.38
Demand equated with the employed female population	--	--	--	0.83	1.22	2.18

[a]Does not include girls 18-19 years old enrolled in school.

Sources: Derived from Tables 5.7 and 5.9 above.

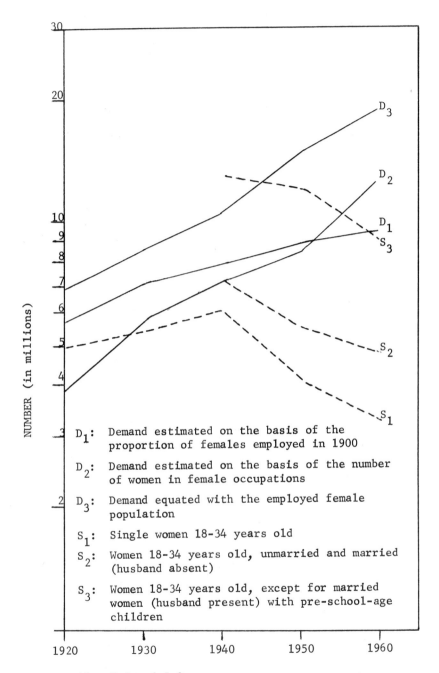

D_1: Demand estimated on the basis of the proportion of females employed in 1900

D_2: Demand estimated on the basis of the number of women in female occupations

D_3: Demand equated with the employed female population

S_1: Single women 18-34 years old

S_2: Women 18-34 years old, unmarried and married (husband absent)

S_3: Women 18-34 years old, except for married women (husband present) with pre-school-age children

Sources: Tables 5.7 and 5.9.

As a consequence, the supply of young single women in 1960 was far below even the lowest estimate of demand at that date. The low estimate of demand (based on estimated employment in 1900) was three times the size of the pool of single women 18-34 years old. It was obvious that, entirely aside from the work propensities of young single women, it had become impossible for this group to supply a major portion of the female workers in the United States. In general, then, if the female labor force was to grow in the postwar period, it was clear that this increase was not going to be supplied by a declining segment of the population. Employers were going to have to start utilizing other groups in the female population.

We have data to construct the second pool of young women for the 1940-1960 period only. Although this pool excludes only those women in the 18-34 age group who were married and living with their husbands, it was much too small to provide a source of supply equal to any of the three estimates of demand in either 1950 or 1960. As with the first pool, this source of supply had become increasingly inadequate since 1940.

The last pool of young women excludes only those married women (husbands present) who are also mothers of pre-school-age children--those women under the greatest obligation to stay in the home. Again we have data for the 1940-1960 period only. An interesting characteristic of this pool is that in 1940 it was large enough to cover all three estimates of the demand for female labor. In 1940, therefore, it was still practical for employers to prefer young women, because there were enough of them around to provide a major portion of the female labor force, even if all of them did not work. However, this pool, like the others, declined in the 1940-1960 period, and by 1960 it was below all three estimates of demand. The ratio of the minimum estimate of demand to this pool was 1.10 in 1960; of the maximum estimate, 2.18.

In general, then, it is clear that in the 1940-1960 period--the time which saw the major changes in the age pattern of female labor force participation--there was a steady decline in the supply of young women, regardless of any changes in their work propensities. As a consequence, the expansion of the female labor force in the 1940-1960 period depended on the increased utilization of older women. In fact, it would have been impossible even to have maintained 1940 employment levels without turning more to older women. Thus, to the extent that the maintenance and expansion of the female labor force depended on an increased utilization of older women, employer preferences for young women (or young single women) became increasingly unrealistic in the postwar period. Here, then, is good evidence of a growing divergence in supply and demand to back up the evidence presented in Chapter 4 suggesting that a major reason for shifts in hiring policies with respect to the age of female workers was the growing shortage of young women.

The Demand for Female Labor and the Supply of Women 18-64 Years Old. When we examine the trend in the pool of women 18-64 years old who were single, widowed, or divorced, we see that up to 1940 this pool was increasing (Table 5.14 and Chart 5.10), though not as rapidly as the two higher estimates of demand. In 1940 the pool was still large enough to cover all the estimates of demand. Therefore, it was still practical to count on women who were not married to contribute the majority of female workers, provided a fairly substantial proportion of them worked. However, after 1940, the supply of such women declined--15 percent between 1940 and 1960. As a consequence, in 1960 the number barely matched the minimum estimate of demand and was well below the other two estimates. The maximum estimate--the employed female population in 1960--was almost twice as large as this pool.

In general, it is clear that even if all unmarried women in the broad age group of 18-64 had been available for employment, the number would hardly have been sufficient to produce the 1940-1960 expansion in female employment. However, not all these women were available for employment, or could have been induced to enter the labor market.

If we try to be more realistic in our effort to determine the maximum number of women without husbands to support them, and add married women with husbands absent to our pool of unmarried women 18-64 years old, the supply of females is somewhat increased. However, this pool also declined in the 1940-1960 period, and by 1960 the minimum estimate of demand was 78 percent of this pool, the medium estimate was 98 percent, and the maximum estimate was 155 percent. Thus, even if practically all unmarried women and married women not living with their husbands had been employed, the supply of such women would not have been sufficient to meet the growing demand for female labor. The growth in female employment, therefore, required the greater utilization of married women living with their husbands. It is only when we get to the last pool--which includes all women 18-64 years old, with the exception of those 18-19 years old in school and married women with husbands present who also have pre-school-age children--that we have a group large enough to cover easily all our demand estimates.

In sum, even if we could assume a maximum utilization of each of the first five pools (and this is unrealistic, as we have seen), it still would have required an increasing utilization of married women living with their husbands to have achieved the female labor force of 1960.

The Supply and Demand for Educated Women. So far, we have seen that there has been a growing demand for female workers in

Table 5.14

ESTIMATES OF THE SUPPLY OF WOMEN 18-64 YEARS OLD COMPARED TO ESTIMATES OF THE DEMAND FOR FEMALE WORKERS: 1900-1960

(Ratio of demand to supply)

	1900	1920	1930	1940	1950	1960
Single, widowed, and divorced women 18-64 years old[a] as compared to:						
Demand estimated on the basis of the proportion of females employed in 1900	0.58	0.64	0.66	0.66	0.84	0.95
Demand estimated on the basis of the number of females in female occupations	0.38	0.43	0.54	0.60	0.82	1.20
Demand equated with the employed female population	0.58	0.77	0.84	0.89	1.38	1.89
Women 18-64 years old, unmarried and married with husbands absent,[a] as compared to:						
Demand estimated on the basis of the proportion of females employed in 1900	--	--	--	0.59	0.72	0.78
Demand estimated on the basis of the number of females in female occupations	--	--	--	0.54	0.70	0.98
Demand equated with the employed female population	--	--	--	0.80	1.18	1.55
Women 18-64 years old, except for married women (husbands present) with pre-school-age children,[a] as compared to:						
Demand estimated on the basis of the proportion of females employed in 1900	--	--	--	0.24	0.25	0.27
Demand estimated on the basis of the number of females in female occupations	--	--	--	0.22	0.24	0.34
Demand equated with the employed female population	--	--	--	0.32	0.41	0.54

[a]The supply does not include girls 18-19 years old enrolled in school.

Source: Derived from Tables 5.7 and 5.9 above.

CHART 5.10. POOLS OF WOMEN 18-64 YEARS OLD COMPARED TO VARIOUS
ESTIMATES OF THE DEMAND FOR FEMALE WORKERS: 1920-1960

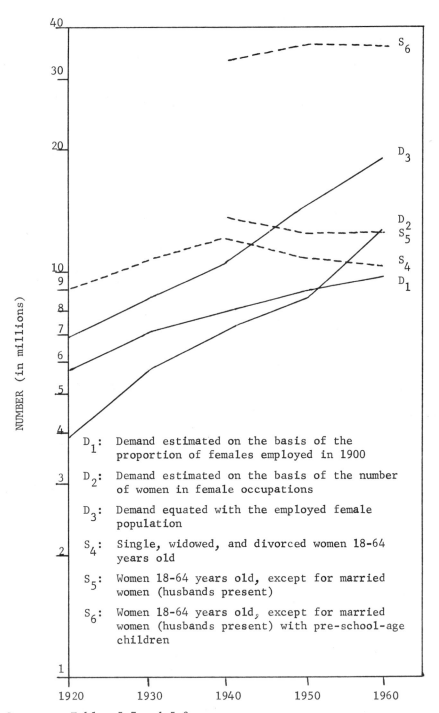

D_1: Demand estimated on the basis of the proportion of females employed in 1900

D_2: Demand estimated on the basis of the number of women in female occupations

D_3: Demand equated with the employed female population

S_4: Single, widowed, and divorced women 18-64 years old

S_5: Women 18-64 years old, except for married women (husbands present)

S_6: Women 18-64 years old, except for married women (husbands present) with pre-school-age children

Sources: Tables 5.7 and 5.9.

the postwar years, but a decreasing supply of the kind of worker typical of the prewar period. The increasing demand for female workers has been greatest for the more educated woman. The growth in employment has, after all, been most pronounced in white-collar occupations--particularly professional and clerical occupations (Table 5.4). Has the divergence in supply and demand which we have observed for women at all skill levels also been character- istic of the better educated worker? The data relevant to this question are relatively scarce; nevertheless, we should be able to get a rough idea of the situation for 1950 and 1960 at least. First, however, we must decide how to estimate the supply and demand for educated female labor--for women who had, at the very minimum, completed high school.

There is no a priori way of determining in which jobs em- ployers require women with a high school education or better, and in which jobs they get such women more or less by accident. How- ever, it seems quite certain that professional and clerical occu- pations generally demand better educated women. In addition, many specific occupations within the other general occupational categories probably also require educated workers. However, we will ignore these, and take for our estimate of demand only those females in professional and clerical occupations who have com- pleted at least four years of high school.

On the supply side, we can construct two pools for both 1950 and 1960 of potential female workers with this educational attainment: (1) single, widowed, divorced, and married women (husband absent) who were 18-34 years old, and (2) women in the same marital status categories who were in the broader 18-64 age group. For 1960 we can construct pools of women 18-34 and 18-64 years old which include, in addition to the women listed above, married women without pre-school-age children.

In both 1950 and 1960, the number of women with a high school education or better who were in professional and clerical occupations (our estimate of demand) greatly exceeded the esti- mate of the supply of better educated young women who were un- married or married with husbands absent (Table 5.15). This discrepancy between supply and demand increased considerably in the 1950-1960 period. As a consequence, in 1960 the demand for better educated young women was over twice as large as the estimate of the supply of such women. Nor was the pool of young women, when expanded to include married women without pre-school- age children, large enough to cover the estimate of demand in 1960. There is thus considerable evidence that a general short- age of young women relative to demand existed for the more edu- cated workers, as well as for all female workers. This finding is particularly significant when we remember that hiring policies unfavorable to married women or older women were most character- istic of, as well as best documented for, the professional and

Table 5.15

THE DEMAND FOR AND SUPPLY OF EDUCATED FEMALE WORKERS:
1950 AND 1960

Supply of better educated females in different marital-status groups[a]	Demand for better educated females as a ratio of the supply[a]	
	1950	1960
Women 18-34 years old		
Single, widowed, divorced, and married (husband absent)	1.48	2.09
Single, widowed, divorced, married (husband absent) and married (husband present) with no children under six	--[b]	1.24
Women 18-64 years old		
Single, widowed, divorced, and married (husband absent)	0.89	1.15
Single, widowed, divorced, married (husband absent) and married (husband present) with no children under six	--[b]	0.44

[a]"Better educated" females are those women with at least four years of high school. The demand for such women was estimated by taking the number of female professional and clerical workers at this level of educational attainment.

[b]Not available.

Sources: Derived from U.S. Bureau of the Census, 1950 Census of Population: Special Report No. P-E No. 5B, Education, Table 8, and Special Report P-E No. 1B, Occupational Characteristics, Table 10; 1960 Census of Population: Subject Report PC(2)-5B, Educational Attainment, Table 5, and Subject Report PC(2)-7A, Occupational Characteristics, Table 9.

clerical occupations--the occupations which provide the basis of this estimate of demand.

If we compare the pool of unmarried women plus married women with husbands absent, expanded to include women 18-64 years old and not just those 18-34 years old, we see that demand was slightly below supply in 1950, but not in 1960. Again, it is only when we add women without pre-school-age children that we arrive at a supply greatly in excess of demand.

In general, then, the supply of the more educated female workers of an age and with family characteristics most typical of the prewar worker was not keeping up with the demand for such workers in the 1950-1960 period. The results of our study of women at the upper educational levels are not very different, therefore, from the results of our analysis of women at all educational levels combined.

The Interaction of Supply and Demand. What are the implications of our comparison of the trends in the demand for female labor with the trends in the supply of the kind of women who provided the typical workers of the prewar period? As far as demand is concerned, we have seen that all three of our estimates indicate a rising demand for female labor, particularly since 1940. This is perhaps most significant in the case of the second series of estimates, which is based on the number of women in predominantly female occupations, and hence is not directly dependent on population growth.

With regard to the supply of the typical worker of 1900, it is obvious that while there were enough single women to have provided the major source of labor in 1900, this group was much too small a proportion of the total female population to permit any significant expansion in the female labor force. Even if the supply of young single women had remained at the 1900 level, this pool would have been well below all three of the estimates of demand in either 1950 or 1960 (Table 5.13 and Chart 5.9). Of course, the pool of young single women did not remain at the 1900 level throughout the 1900-1960 period. It increased somewhat from 1900 to 1940, and then declined so sharply that it was smaller in 1960 than in 1900.

There were really two kinds of women typical of the female labor force in 1940--young women (59 percent of the female labor force was under 35) and women without husbands (70.4 percent of the female labor force was single, widowed, divorced, or married with husbands absent). As far as the young worker is concerned, the analysis shows that there was a growing shortage of young women in the 1940-1960 period. The postwar expansion in the female labor force, therefore, rested on the increased employment of older women. In addition, the supply of women 18-64 years old who were not married, or who were married with husbands absent, was also declining in the postwar period. Hence the expansion of the female labor force rested not only on an increased utilization of older women, but also on an increased utilization of married women with husbands present.

All this lends weight to the argument that a greatly increased supply was not the dominant and initiating factor in the large postwar growth of the older married female labor force. It seems suspiciously fortuitous, after all, that just as the supply of the typical worker of 1940 and earlier was declining, the supply of older married women to the labor force was, for entirely different reasons, rising. A much more reasonable explanation is that the combination of the rising demand for female labor and the declining supply of the typical worker opened up job opportunities for married women and older women that had not previously existed. As we have seen, there is substantial evidence from data on hiring policies that precisely this has occurred, for discrimination against married women and older women has declined markedly in the postwar period. If this reasoning is valid, then the great influx of older married women into the labor force was, in good part, a response to increased job opportunities--not a creator of such opportunities. The greater availability of labor-saving products and services may have facilitated this response, but it did not initiate it.

Conclusion

This chapter represents the culmination of our investigation of the reasons for the 1940-1960 changes in female labor force participation. The objective has been to put the role of economic and demographic factors into proper perspective--first, with respect to the rise in the total female work rate, and second, with respect to the rise in the work rates of older women and married women.

The Rise in the Total Work Rate. The basic industrial and occupational shifts experienced in our society in the course of its economic development have led, on balance, to a rise in the demand for female labor--a rise that has been particularly marked in the 1940-1960 period. This growth in demand has been due primarily to the fact that the most rapidly expanding industries and occupations have for some time been major employers of women.

Since there is evidence that the supply of female labor is responsive to labor demand, the most likely explanation of the postwar rise in the female work rate is that an increasing number of women have been drawn into the labor force in response to an expansion in job opportunities. In other words, it appears that demand has been the dominant factor in the situation, and supply has adjusted itself to demand. However, because a moderate growth in the female labor force as a whole has depended on a very rapid growth in the work propensities of particular kinds of women, the situation is more complicated than this view suggests. We must look to the explanation of the rise in the work rates of older married women to understand the kind of interaction between economic and demographic factors which was taking place.

The Rise in the Work Rates of Older Women and Married Women. When we examine the rising work rates of older women and married women, it becomes clear that the kind of interaction between economic and demographic factors which is involved is rather complex. The women who used to provide the backbone of the American female labor force--the unmarried and the young--constituted a stationary or declining population group in the 1940-1960 period. As a consequence, the only way a rising demand for female labor could have been met was by the increased employment of older married women. We can, then, view the entry into the labor force of older married women as a response to increased job opportunities-- in other words, they were responding to an increased demand for their labor. This argument is bolstered by recent research which shows that the supply of labor, and of female labor in particular, is quite responsive to shifts in the demand for labor. Further supporting evidence comes from studies of hiring practices. These have indicated a rather marked decline in discriminatory hiring policies directed at married women or older women. If only because of this evidence, it does not seem reasonable to subscribe to the view that the rise in the work rates of older married women has resulted primarily from the influence of supply factors operating independently of the demand for labor. In addition, we have seen in Chapter 2 that the effects of supply factors operating independently of demand give little support to the supply hypothesis.

On the other hand, it should be clear that it is a mistake to rely too heavily on demand as the explanatory factor. Given the shifting sizes of the various population groups from which female labor is supplied, it is not realistic to argue that these shifts were irrelevant to the changes in female labor force participation. That something more complex than a simple rise in demand was involved is indicated by the great increases in the work rates among women who had not traditionally been a major segment of the female labor force and for whom, presumably, there was not an established demand. To the extent that this is true, it seems more satisfactory to explain the rise in the demand for such labor as a response to shortages of young women or single women, rather than as due to a mysterious change of heart among employers.

In sum, the evidence indicates that the best explanation for the great increases in the work rates of older married women is that while the demand for female labor had been rising, the supply of the more preferred type of female labor was declining. In response to this declining supply, demand readjusted itself, so that workers who used to be discriminated against were now acceptable and, perhaps, even sought after. In turn, this broadening of the demand for female labor led to a responsive increase in the supply of older married women to the labor market. In general, then, we have had a decline in the supply of two kinds of female workers--the young woman and the single woman--because of a decline in the population groups from which that labor was drawn. We have had, on the other hand, an increase in the supply of two other kinds of female workers--the older woman and the married woman--because the work propensities of such women have risen in response to an expanding demand for their labor. As a consequence of the rapid growth of the older married female labor force, the female labor force as a whole has been able to achieve a moderate growth in the postwar period.

Abbott, Edith. _Women in Industry_. New York: D. Appleton & Co.,
1910.

Axelson, Leland J. "The Marital Adjustment and Marital Role
Definitions of Husbands of Working and Nonworking Wives,"
Marriage and Family Living, 25 (May 1963), pp. 189-195.

Bancroft, Gertrude. _The American Labor Force_. New York: John
Wiley and Sons, Inc., 1958.

_____. "Labor Force Growth and Job Opportunities: Some
Doctrines and the Evidence," _Exploring the Dimensions of the
Manpower Revolution_, Vol. I: _Selected Readings in Employment
and Manpower_. U.S. Senate, Committee on Labor and Public
Welfare, Subcommittee on Employment and Manpower, 88th
Congress, 2nd Session. Washington, 1964.

Bestor, Arthur. _Restoration of Learning_. New York: Alfred A.
Knopf, 1955.

Bowen, William G. and Finegan, T.A. "Labor Force Participation
and Unemployment," _Employment Policy and the Labor Market_,
ed. Arthur M. Ross. Berkeley: University of California
Press, 1965.

Cain, Glenn. _Married Women in the Labor Force_. Chicago: University of Chicago Press, 1966.

Cantril, Hadley. _Public Opinion, 1935-1946_. Princeton: Princeton University Press, 1951.

Caplow, Theodore. _The Sociology of Work_. Minneapolis: University of Minnesota Press, 1954.

Centers, Richard. _The Psychology of Social Classes_. Princeton:
Princeton University Press, 1949.

Clark, Colin. _The Conditions of Economic Progress_. 3rd edition.
London: Macmillan & Co., 1947.

Collver, Andrew, and Langlois, Eleanor. "The Female Labor Force
in Metropolitan Areas: An International Comparison," _Eco-
nomic Development and Cultural Change_, X (July 1962), pp. 367-
385.

"Discrimination in Employment or Occupation on the Basis of Marital Status: I," International Labour Review, LXXXV (March 1962), pp. 262-282.

"Discrimination in Employment or Occupation on the Basis of Marital Status: II," International Labour Review, LXXXV (April 1962), pp. 368-389.

Douglas, Paul H. The Theory of Wages. New York: The Macmillan Co., 1934.

Douglas, Paul H., and Schoenberg, Erika H. "Studies in the Supply Curve of Labor," Journal of Political Economy, 45 (February 1937), pp. 45-79.

Durand, John D. The Labor Force in the United States, 1890-1960. New York: Social Science Research Council, 1948.

Editors of Fortune. The Executive Life. Garden City, New York: Doubleday & Co., 1956. [Dolphin Books.]

Edwards, Alba M. Comparative Occupation Statistics for the United States, 1870 to 1940. U.S. Bureau of the Census, 1943.

Giedion, Siegfried. Mechanization Takes Command. New York: Oxford University Press, 1948.

Ginder, Charles E. "Chapter Surveys Give Comparative Data on Discrimination Against Older Workers in New York, San Francisco, Houston," Office Executive, 33 (October 1958), p. 43.

_____. "Factor of Sex in Office Employment," Office Executive, 36 (February 1961), pp. 10-13.

Gitlow, A.L. Labor Economics and Industrial Relations. Homewood, Ill.: Richard D. Irwin, Inc., 1957.

Glick, Paul C. American Families. New York: John Wiley and Sons, Inc., 1957.

Gordon, Margaret S. "U.S. Manpower and Employment Policy," Monthly Labor Review, 87 (November 1964), pp. 1314-1321.

Grabill, Wilson H., Kiser, Clyde V., and Whelpton, Pascal K. The Fertility of American Women. New York: John Wiley and Sons, Inc., 1958.

Haber, S. "Female Labor Force Participation and Economic Development," Rand Corporation [Paper] P-1504. Santa Monica, California: Rand Corporation, 1958.

Hiestand, Dale L. Economic Growth and Employment Opportunities for Minorities. New York: Columbia University Press, 1964.

Hussey, Miriam. Personnel Policies During a Period of Shortage of Young Women Workers in Philadelphia. Industrial Research Unit, Wharton School of Finance and Commerce, University of Pennsylvania, 1958.

Jaffe, A.J. "Trends in the Participation of Women in the Working Force," Monthly Labor Review, LXXIX (May 1956), pp. 559-565.

Jaffe, A.J., and Stewart, C.D. Manpower Resources and Utilization. New York: John Wiley and Sons, Inc., 1951.

Kaplan D.L., and Casey, M. Claire. Occupational Trends in the United States, 1900 to 1950. U.S. Bureau of the Census, Working Paper No. 5, 1958.

Kerr, Clark. "The Balkanization of Labor Markets," Labor Mobility and Economic Opportunity, ed. E. Weight Bakke et al. New York: John Wiley and Sons, Inc., 1954.

Koerner, James. Miseducation of American Teachers. Boston: Houghton Mifflin, 1963.

Kyrk, Hazel. "Who Works and Why," Women's Opportunities and Responsibilities: Annals of the American Academy of Political and Social Science, 251 (May 1947), pp. 44-52.

Lebergott, Stanley. Manpower in Economic Growth. New York: McGraw-Hill Book Co., Inc., 1964.

Leibenstein, Harvey. Economic Backwardness and Economic Growth. New York: John Wiley and Sons, Inc., 1957.

Leiter, Sara. "Hiring Policies, Prejudices, and the Older Worker," Monthly Labor Review, 88 (August 1965), pp. 968-970.

Long, Clarence D. The Labor Force Under Changing Income and Employment. National Bureau of Economic Research. Princeton: Princeton University Press, 1958.

Manpower Report of the President and a Report on Manpower Requirements, Resources, Utilization, and Training. U.S. Department of Labor, 1963.

Mason, Ward S. The Beginning Teacher. U.S. Department of Health, Education and Welfare, Office of Education. Circular No. 644. Washington, 1961.

Mincer, Jacob. "Labor Force Participation of Married Women: A

Study of Labor Supply," in National Bureau of Economic Research, Aspects of Labor Economics. Princeton: Princeton University Press, 1962.

Morgan, James N. et al. Income and Welfare in the United States. New York: McGraw-Hill Book Co., Inc., 1962.

National Education Association. "Administrative Practices Affecting Classroom Teachers, Part I: The Selection and Appointment of Teachers," Research Bulletin, X (January 1932), pp. 1-33.

_____. "Practices Affecting Teacher Personnel," Research Bulletin, 6 (September 1928), pp. 208-254.

_____. "Teacher Personnel Procedures: Selection and Appointment," Research Bulletin, XX (March 1942), pp. 51-79.

_____. "Teacher Personnel Practices, 1950-51: Appointment and Termination of Service," Research Bulletin, XXX (February 1952), pp. 1-31.

National Manpower Council. Womanpower. New York: Columbia University Press, 1957.

Noland, E.W., and Bakke, E.W. Workers Wanted: A Study of Employers' Hiring Policies, Preferences, and Practices in New Haven and Charlotte. New York: Harper & Bros., 1949.

Palmer, Gladys L. Labor Mobility in Six Cities. New York: Social Science Research Council, 1954.

Parnes, Herbert S. Research on Labor Mobility: An Appraisal of Research Findings in the United States. New York: Social Science Research Council, 1954.

Peters, David W. The Status of the Married Woman Teacher. New York: Bureau of Publications, Teachers College, Columbia University, 1934.

Reynolds, Lloyd G. The Structure of Labor Markets. New York: Harper and Bros., 1951.

Rossi, Alice S. "Women in Science: Why So Few?" Science, 148 (May 28, 1965), pp. 1196-1202.

Shallcross, Ruth. Should Married Women Work? Public Affairs Pamphlet No. 49, 1940.

Smuts, Robert W. "The Female Labor Force: A Case Study in the Interpretation of Historical Statistics," Journal of the American Statistical Association, LV (March 1960), pp. 71-79.

SELECTED BIBLIOGRAPHY

_____. Women and Work in America. New York: Columbia
University Press, 1959.

Stigler, George. Trends in Employment in the Service Industries.
National Bureau of Economic Research. Princeton: Princeton
University Press, 1956.

Stirling, Betty. "The Interrelation of Changing Attitudes and
Changing Conditions with Reference to the Labor Force Participation of Wives." Unpublished doctoral dissertation.
Department of Sociology, University of California, Berkeley,
1963.

Tella, Alfred. "The Relation of Labor Force to Employment,"
Industrial and Labor Relations Review, 17 (April 1964), pp.
454-469.

U.S. Bureau of the Census. 1910 Census of Population: Vol. IV,
Population: Occupation Statistics.

_____. 1930 Census of Population: Vol. V, General Report
on Occupations.

_____. 1940 Census of Population: Vol. III, The Labor Force.

_____. 1940 Census of Population: The Labor Force (Sample
Statistics), "Employment and Family Characteristics of Women."

_____. 1950 Census of Population: Vol. II, Characteristics
of the Population, Part 1, U.S. Summary.

_____. 1950 Census of Population: Vol. IV, Special Reports,
Part 1, Chapter B, "Occupational Characteristics."

_____. 1950 Census of Population: Vol. IV, Special Reports,
Part 5, Chapter B, "Education."

_____. 1950 Census of Population: Vol. IV, Special Reports,
Part 5, Chapter C, "Fertility."

_____. 1960 Census of Population: Vol. I, Characteristics
of the Population, Part 2, U.S. Summary.

_____. 1960 Census of Population: Subject Report PC(2)-6A,
Employment Status and Work Experience.

_____. 1960 Census of Population: Subject Report PC(2)-7A,
Occupational Characteristics.

_____. 1960 Census of Population: Subject Report PC(2)-5B,
Educational Attainment.

_____. *1960 Census of Population:* Subject Report PC(2)-7C, Occupation by Industry.

_____. *1960 Census of Population:* Selected Area Reports, No. PC(3)-1D, Standard Metropolitan Statistical Areas.

_____. *Current Population Reports,* Series P-25, No. 286, "Projections of the Population of the United States, by Age and Sex: 1964 to 1985."

_____. *Current Population Reports,* Series P-50, No. 39, "Marital and Family Characteristics of the Labor Force in the United States: April 1951."

_____. *Historical Statistics of the United States:* Colonial Times to 1957.

_____. *Historical Statistics of the United States:* Continuation to 1962 and Revisions.

_____. *Statistical Abstract of the United States, 1964.*

U.S. Bureau of Labor Statistics. *Special Labor Force Report,* No. 31, "Labor Force and Employment, 1960-62."

_____. *Special Labor Force Report,* No. 35, "Job Mobility in 1961."

_____. *Special Labor Force Report,* No. 40, "Marital and Family Characteristics of Workers, March 1963."

U.S. Department of Labor. Women's Bureau. *Careers for Women as Technicians.* Bulletin No. 282. Washington, 1962.

_____. *Economic Indicators Relating to Equal Pay.* Pamphlet 9. Washington, 1963.

_____. *First Jobs of College Women:* Report of Women Graduates, Class of 1957. Bulletin No. 168. Washington, 1959.

_____. *1962 Handbook of Women Workers.* Bulletin No. 285. Washington, 1963.

Whyte, William F. "The Social Structure of the Restaurant," *American Journal of Sociology,* LIV (January 1949), pp. 302-310.

Williams, Josephine. "Patients and Prejudice: Lay Attitudes Toward Women Physicians," *American Journal of Sociology,* 51 (January 1946), pp. 283-287.

SELECTED BIBLIOGRAPHY

Woody, Thomas. A History of Women's Education in the United States, Vol. I. New York: The Science Press, 1929.

"The World's Working Population: Its Distribution by Status and Occupation," International Labour Review, LXXIV (August 1956), pp. 174-192.

"The World's Working Population: Its Industrial Distribution," International Labour Review, LXXIII (May 1956), pp. 501-521.